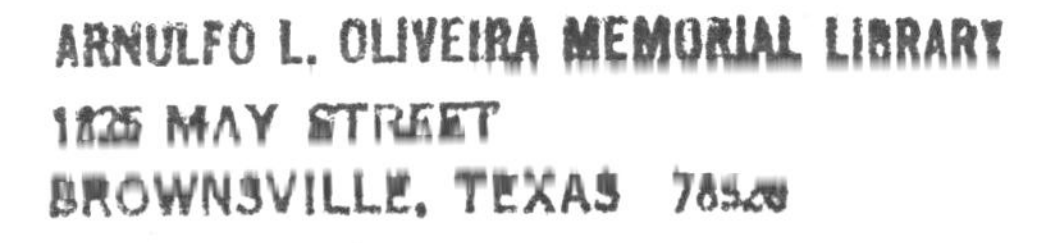
ARNULFO L. OLIVEIRA MEMORIAL LIBRARY
1825 MAY STREET
BROWNSVILLE, TEXAS

A Citizen's Guide to the New Tax Reforms

A Citizen's Guide to the New Tax Reforms

Fair Tax, Flat Tax, Simple Tax

Edited by
Joseph A. Pechman

ROWMAN & ALLANHELD
PUBLISHERS

ROWMAN & ALLANHELD

Published in the United States of America in 1985
by Rowman & Allanheld, Publishers
(a division of Littlefield, Adams & Company)
81 Adams Drive, Totowa, New Jersey 07512

Library of Congress Cataloging in Publication Data
Main entry under title:

A Citizen's guide to the new tax reforms.

Includes index.
1. Income tax—Law and legislation—United States.
2. Flat-rate income tax—United States. 3. Taxation
of articles of consumption—United States.
I. Pechman, Joseph A., 1918–
KF6369.C58 1985 343.7305′2 84-24806
ISBN 0-8476-7403-7 347.30352
ISBN 0-8476-7404-5 (pbk.)

85 86 87 / 10 9 8 7 6 5 4 3 2 1

Printed in the United States of America

Contents

1 Introduction

Joseph A. Pechman

The federal tax system is in disarray today. It is widely believed to be unfair, because many people pay tax on their entire income, while others pay on only part of their income or not at all. It imposes heavy taxes on some firms and industries while subsidizing others. The resulting distortions reduce the productivity of the economy and make everyone worse off. The tax has also become very complicated—so much so that few people can fill out their own tax returns, and many are forced to pay fees to private firms to prepare them. Finally, federal taxes do not raise nearly enough revenue to balance the budget. High interest rates and the overvalued dollar are caused at least in part by inadequate tax collections.

This deplorable state of affairs is not something that has emerged only recently. It has been developing for a long time. The modern income tax, which was enacted in 1913, originally had a number of unnecessary deductions that remain in the law and cost the federal government billions of dollars. But Congress has added to the list of tax favors in almost every tax bill enacted since then, and of late it is doing so with increasing frequency.

One consequence of this practice is that the tax return has become more and more complicated. The 1983 tax return contained, in addition to an initial two-page summary, nine separate schedules and thirty-five supplementary forms to report details of income receipts, deductions, and tax credits. On the two-page summary, eight adjustments were allowed in calculating adjusted gross income and seven tax credits were provided. In 1960 there was only one adjustment to calculate adjusted gross income and one tax credit.

The law itself has become completely incomprehensible to all but a few specialized tax lawyers and accountants. Every tax bill in recent years has been hundreds of pages long (the 1984 bill was more than 1,000 pages), partly because Congress has been trying to close a few of the most egregious tax loopholes, but also because it continues to open up new ones almost every year. Under the circumstances, there is widespread agreement that something needs to be done to clean up the income tax. The idea is to start all over again—eliminate all or most of the unnecessary tax preferences and use the revenue so generated to reduce the tax rates. Comprehensive income taxation along these lines is not a new idea (it goes back at least fifty years to a University of Chicago economist named Henry Simons), but it has gained a good deal of momentum as more and more people have become fed up. The idea has been nurtured in the intervening years by a few tax theorists, but it achieved considerable prominence only when a number of key politicians climbed on the bandwagon.

The latest converts to comprehensive income taxation are people who would substitute one rate, often called a flat rate, for the system of graduated rates we have had from the beginning. The flat tax is supposed to simplify things even further (which is true), but it would also redistribute the tax burden from the wealthy to the low- and middle-income groups.

COMPREHENSIVE INCOME TAXATION

The essence of comprehensive income taxation is to tax all incomes without any exclusions, personal deductions (except for unusual expenses that reduce ability to pay), or tax credits. The broadened tax base would then be used to reduce tax rates across the board. Taxpayers would simply add up all income, subtract their personal exemptions and unusual expenses, and calculate their tax from a tax table or the schedule of tax rates.

The advantages of such a system are obvious. First, it would treat people with the same income and family responsibilities in the same way. Today, there are vast differences in the tax paid by people who are in essentially the same economic circumstances. Under a truly comprehensive income tax, these "horizontal inequities" would be wiped out and the tax rates would truly reflect the degree of graduation, or "vertical" equity, of the tax system.

Second, the reduction in tax rates and the broadened tax base would improve economic efficiency. Although economists do not know precisely how much the increase would be, lower tax rates would increase incentives to work, save, and invest and reduce the incentive to cheat. Furthermore, the distortions arising from the differential tax rates on different investments would be eliminated and productivity would be improved. Uneconomic investments that yielded only an after-tax profit would no longer be profitable. In effect, the nation can have a free lunch—higher economic growth—merely by eliminating the discriminatory features of the tax law. The increase in growth would be much more modest than the supply-side economists have suggested, but even a modest increase would be welcome.

Third, the tax law and tax returns would be greatly simplified and the costs of administration and compliance would be cut drastically. Elimination of the tax preferences and unnecessary deductions would automatically eliminate most of the supplementary schedules taxpayers are required to file today. The tax return itself could be put comfortably on one page. (Some allege that it could be compressed to postcard size, but this would mean that some information now on page one of the return, such as the backup for personal exemptions, would be relegated to a supplementary schedule.) Above all, comprehensive income taxation would make it possible for all taxpayers to understand the income tax and to prepare their own tax returns, if they wished to do so. Many of the people who now make a living advising taxpayers on how to reduce their taxes and preparing tax returns would be forced to devote their energies to other activities.

A comprehensive tax base would conform as closely as possible to an economic concept of income. In addition to adjusted gross income as now defined on the first page of the tax return, income under a comprehensive tax would include capital gains in full, interest on newly issued state and local government bonds, interest on life insurance savings, Social Security, and railroad retirement benefits in excess of the amounts contributed through the employee tax, Workers' Compensation, unemployment benefits, veterans payments, and fringe benefits (such as premiums on health insurance plans). Deductions for individual retirement plans (IRAs) would be limited to those not covered by pension plans. In computing the tax base for a business enterprise, whether incorporated or unincorporated, all net profits would be taxed. Accelerated depreciation and the investment tax credit now allowed for plant and equipment spending would be eliminated. Personal deductions would be limited to unusual medical expenses and casualty losses (say, those in excess of 10 percent of income) because they reduce ability to pay. To be sure that costs of investment are properly accounted for, interest payments on debt would be deductible only to the extent that the taxpayer reported any investment income; the rest would be carried forward against investment income in future years.

This definition of the income tax base is of course only a purist's dream. Few of the comprehensive tax proposals now being discussed would go that far, but all of them would move in that direction, and their broadened tax bases would permit rate reductions of 40 percent or more. The top individual income tax rate could be reduced from 50 percent to 30 percent or less, and the corporate rate could be cut from 46 percent at least to the same 30 percent. Thus it isn't necessary to be a purist to be able to make deep cuts in the tax rates.

THE FLAT TAX

The original idea of a comprehensive income tax was to maintain a system of graduated tax rates, but at reduced levels. The flat taxers added a new wrinkle: Instead of a multiple-rate system, they propose to use only a single rate. Like the graduated system, the flat rate would be chosen to yield the same revenue raised by the present income tax. The exact rate needed to come out even depends on the amounts added to the tax base and the personal exemptions. The broader the tax base and the lower the personal exemptions, the lower the tax rate. In practice, most of the flat-tax systems that have been proposed would have a rate somewhere between 15 and 20 percent.

The objective of all comprehensive income tax proposals, whether combined with graduated rates or a flat rate, is to keep the progressivity of the tax system approximately the same as it is under present law. (A *progressive* tax rises as a percentage of income as income rises; a *regressive* tax falls as a percentage of income as income rises; and a *proportional* tax is the same percentage of income in all income classes.) I have calculated that this can be done with nine brackets instead of the fourteen now used and rates ranging from 9 percent in the bottom bracket to 28 percent in the top bracket. In making the calculation, I assumed that the exemptions would be raised from $1,000 to $1,750 per capita and that the standard deduction (now called the zero bracket) would be increased from $2,300 for single persons and $3,400 for married couples to $4,000 per capita. The increase in exemptions is needed to raise the minimum taxable

Table 1.1 *Effective Tax Rates Under Present Law and Under a Comprehensive Income Tax Using Alternative Tax-Rate Plans, by Income Class, 1984*

Income classes in thousands of dollars; rates in percent

		Alternative plan[a]	
Expanded adjusted gross income class[b]	*Present law*	*Graduated rates, 9–28 percent*[c]	*Flat Tax rate, 17 percent*
0–5,000	0.7	0.0	0.0
5,000–10,000	4.0	1.6	3.0
10,000–15,000	6.0	4.2	7.1
15,000–20,000	7.7	6.5	9.2
20,000–25,000	9.1	8.3	10.6
25,000–35,000	10.0	10.0	11.8
35,000–50,000	11.4	12.4	13.0
50,000–100,000	15.5	16.3	14.2
100,000–500,000	23.0	22.1	15.4
500,000–1,000,000	26.4	25.4	15.9
1,000,000 and over	23.1	26.4	16.2
All classes[c]	12.0	12.0	12.0

Source: Joseph A. Pechman and John Karl Scholz, "Comprehensive Income Taxation and Rate Reduction," *Tax Notes*, 17 (11 October 1982), Brookings Reprint 390.

a. Assumes zero-bracket amount of $4,000 and exemption of $1,750 per capita, plus an additional $1,750 for heads of households under both plans.

b. Adjusted gross income plus sick pay, excluded capital gains and dividends, interest on life insurance and state and local bond interest, all unemployment benefits, 50 percent of Social Security benefits, Worker's Compensation, veterans' benefits, tax preferences reported for purposes of the minimum tax, one-third of employer-provided health insurance, employer-provided life insurance, and IRA deductions by those covered under private pension plans.

c. Rates are the same for all marital statuses: They rise from 9 percent on taxable income of less than $5,000 to 28 percent on the amount of taxable income in excess of $150,000. Married couples with two earners would receive a deduction of 25 percent of the earnings of the spouse with the lower earnings (for earnings up to $50,000).

level to the poverty line, a policy that Congress followed throughout most of the 1970s but forgot in its zeal to enact the Reagan 23 percent tax cuts.

The effect of this tax on the distribution of tax burdens is shown in Table 1.1. The first column shows the average percentage of income paid in tax in the various income classes under present law. This percentage increases from 0.7 for those with income of less than $5,000 to a maximum of 26.4 for those with incomes of $500,000 to $1 million. It then declines to 23.1 for those with income of $1 million or more. The decline is the result of the reduced rate on capital gains, which make up a very large proportion of income in the $1 million class.

With such a comprehensive tax, the average tax paid would begin at zero in the bottom class and rise to 26.1 percent in the top class. The average tax rates in all income classes are fairly close to the present-law rates in all income classes (it is impossible to come out absolutely the same in all classes), except at the bottom, where the higher personal exemptions reduce tax burdens. A smaller number of tax-rate brackets could be used, but the approximation would not be as good. The revenue is the same as under present law because the average tax rate for all income classes combined is the same 12 percent.

Now compare what happens to tax burdens when a flat tax is substituted for the graduated rates (see the second column of Table 1). The rate needed to raise the same revenue is 17 percent. The percentage of income paid under the flat tax increases from zero in the bottom class to only 16.2 percent in the top class (as compared to a maximum of 26.4 percent in the graduated system). Since the revenue is the same under both systems, the tax reduction enjoyed by the very rich must be raised from those with lower incomes. In fact, as Table 1.1 shows, the breaking point is at the $50,000 income level. Above that level, the average tax is lower under the flat tax than under present law and lower than under the comprehensive system with graduated rates. Below that level, the average tax paid is higher under the flat tax.

The flat taxers argue that their system has two advantages. First, the flat tax reduces complexity. Flat taxes avoid bracket creep and thus eliminate the need for adjusting the tax brackets for inflation and for averaging to smoothe out fluctuations in income. They also eliminate the marriage penalty on two-earner couples. These are real simplifications, but they are purchased at the expense of a considerable redistribution of tax burdens from the rich to the low- and middle-income classes.

Second, the flat taxers argue that the reduction in marginal tax rates would greatly improve economic incentives and raise the rate of growth. This is also true of the graduated system. The question is whether the additional growth that might be promoted by a reduction in the top marginal rate from 50 to 30 or 28 percent is significantly less than a further reduction to 16 percent. In making this judgment, consideration must be given to the obvious point that the flat tax would raise the marginal tax rates in the bottom brackets, thus offsetting the incentive effect at the top at least to some extent. On balance, the economic advantage of a flat tax, if any, is minimal.

A redistribution of tax burdens from the high- to lower-income classes is not an inherent property of the flat tax. Given the range of graduation under the federal income tax, it is arithmetically impossible to approximate the present distribution of tax burdens with a flat tax. However, graduation under the state tax systems stops at much lower levels than under the federal tax. Such taxes can be converted to a flat tax without redistributing tax burdens. For example, the California income tax, which is graduated up to 11 percent beginning at a taxable income of about $50,000 for joint returns, can be approximated by a flat tax of 7 percent. A bipartisan group of state legislators has introduced a comprehensive flat tax in California, and there is considerable support for this tax by conservatives and liberals alike. Thus the movement toward comprehensive income taxation may well have its initial success through the flat tax at the state rather than the federal level.

THE CONSUMPTION TAX

Another way to arrive at comprehensive income taxation is to substitute a graduated tax on consumption expenditures for the present income tax. This tax would apply to total income less saving (plus borrowing). Since the amount remaining is consumption, an income tax can be converted to a consumption tax by refraining from taxing saving. In practice, it is not necessary to estimate saving. The consumption-tax base can be obtained simply by adding to income the amounts withdrawn by the taxpayer from special qualified acounts (like super IRAs) or subtracting from income the amounts invested in these accounts. Because it is necessary to keep track only of the cash flows into and out of these accounts, the consumption tax is also called a cash flow tax.

Whether or not a consumption-tax base is comprehensive depends on the deductions and exclusions that would be allowed. If all or most of the deductions and preferences were carried over from the income tax, the consumption tax would yield less revenue than the present income tax. On the other hand, if the tax were truly comprehensive, the tax rates could be cut substantially below present rates, but not as low as the comprehensive income tax shown in Table 1.1.

Some tax reformers prefer a consumption tax to an income tax because they believe the tax should apply to what individuals take out of the economy (consumption) rather than what they put into it (labor). If all workers consumed what they earned during their lifetimes, there would be no essential difference between a consumption tax and a tax on labor income. The only difference would be in the timing of the tax paid.

Since many do not consume what they earn, there is a big difference between the consumption and income taxes, and the difference applies mainly to high-income persons, who hand down their wealth to their children and grandchildren through gifts and bequests. To omit gifts and bequests from the tax base would give the rich a huge tax break. Some supporters of the consumption tax resolve this issue by including gifts and bequests in the base, but experience with wealth taxation in the United States and other countries suggests that most gifts and bequests would escape taxation, and this would lead to a greater concentration of wealth in the hands of the relatively few.

It should be pointed out that a graduated consumption tax is *not* the same as a sales tax or, in the modern version, a value-added tax. The sales tax is collected *only* at the retail level, whereas a value-added tax is collected as the goods move through the various stages of production and distribution. These broad-based taxes apply at flat rates and make no distinctions among families of different size or income. Because consumption falls as a percentage of income as incomes rise, a sales or value-added tax is ordinarily regressive. Some countries try to alleviate this regressive feature by providing exemptions or lower rates for food, medicine, and other necessities, but in no country is the sales or value-added tax actually progressive. The consumption tax now being proposed as a substitute for the income tax is a tax on *persons,* not on sales. Its virtues are that it can be levied at graduated rates and can make distinctions between different sizes of families.

Despite these virtues, the graduated consumption tax is no panacea. In the first place, most people would be appalled to learn that the consumption tax is really a tax on wages. The old-fashioned tax on income taxes income recipients on their total ability to pay, which includes property income as well as labor income. Second, transition problems arise when a consumption tax is substituted for an income tax. It would be unfair to tax older people on consumption financed by the wealth they accumulated out of after-tax income. Transition rules would need to be developed to avoid double taxation of this sort, but there is no way to trace whether current consumption is financed out of previously taxed or untaxed wealth. The rules would necessarily be arbitrary and create numerous inequities. Third, the consumption tax would tax young and old families more heavily than they are taxed under the income tax, because they tend to borrow or use accumulated wealth in order to consume. Families headed by middle-aged persons, who typically save, would pay less tax. This redistribution of the tax burden, which seems acceptable in a lifetime perspective, may not be acceptable to the average taxpayer, who has a much shorter horizon.

There is no guarantee that the consumption tax Congress might enact would be any more comprehensive than the present income tax. Preferences for different types of investments and deductions for charitable contributions, state and local income, sales and property taxes, and interest payments might be carried over into the consumption tax. If this happened, the hybrid tax that would result would be a monstrosity.

Comprehensive consumption or income taxes would make the tax system much simpler than it is today. The complications arise when unnecessary preferences are introduced. If the two taxes are kept clean, the tax returns can be kept simple, and the cost of compliance and administration would be greatly reduced. The consumption tax is somewhat more complicated than the income tax for the majority of taxpayers and less complicated for persons with investments (mainly higher-income taxpayers) and business firms. The complications under the consumption tax arise because taxpayers would need to account for changes in their assets and debts to measure saving or dissaving, which is unnecessary under the income tax. On the other hand, a cash flow tax would do away with all the problems of measuring depreciation and investment income, which account for most of the legal and accounting problems of the income tax.

THE CORPORATION INCOME TAX

A corporation income tax is needed under our system of taxation. Without it, the corporation would be a vast reservoir of tax avoidances. Individuals could avoid paying individual income tax by simply accumulating income in corporations. Even if they ultimately cashed in their accumulations by selling their stock at a capital gain and these gains were fully taxable, the deferral of tax through the corporation would be extremely valuable.

The corporation income tax has fared even worse than the individual income tax in recent history. At one time, it produced more revenue than the individual income tax. Today, as a result of the numerous tax preferences enacted for specific industries (oil companies, banks, exporters, life insurance companies, and many others), and the generous allowances for plant and equipment spending, the corporation income tax produces only about one-eighth of what the individual income tax produces. Like the individual income tax, the corporation income tax rate gives the impression that the tax is high, but the actual tax paid is modest indeed. In 1982, for example, the general corporation tax rate was 46 percent, but the actual tax collected was only 13 percent of total corporate profits. However, as a result of the many preferences, there are large differences in the taxes paid by different firms and industries. Some are actually subsidized by the tax system, while others pay heavy taxes.

The remedy for this situation is the same as the remedy proposed for the individual income tax: eliminate all the preferences for corporations as well as individuals, and use the revenue so produced to cut the tax rate. Perhaps the most important changes under this comprehensive tax approach would be to eliminate the investment tax credit and to replace the liberal depreciation allowances with actual depreciation. All corporations would be taxed at a uniform rate on their economic profits, thus eliminating the distortions of the present tax.

In principle, there is no need for a corporation tax at all if the tax system is converted from an income tax to a consumption tax. Since the retained profits of corporations are automatically invested (perhaps not wisely, but they are nevertheless invested), they are not consumption subject to tax. In practice, however, most advocates of a consumption tax apply the cash flow concept to corporations as well as to individuals. For corporations, net cash flows are calculated by subtracting from their net profits the amounts that are invested in the business. Such a tax is justified on the ground that some contribution from the corporations to government revenues is appropriate in a modern industrial society. Furthermore, complete elimination of the corporate tax would allow foreign stockholders to escape U.S. taxes entirely.

Whether the corporation tax remains an income tax or is converted to a cash flow tax, the revenues now produced by the corporation tax could be raised with a lower tax rate, provided that all tax preferences are removed. The rate reduction would be much larger under the income tax approach because it would provide a deduction only for the depreciation of capital goods, whereas the cash flow tax would allow a deduction for the full cost of such goods when they are purchased.

ALTERNATIVE PLANS

The objectives of comprehensive income taxation can be achieved in many ways. The chapters by Senator Bill Bradley on the Bradley-Gephardt bill, Congressman Jack Kemp on the Kemp-Kasten bill, Henry J. Aaron and Harvey Galper on a graduated consumption tax, and professors Robert E. Hall and Alvin Rabushka on a flat-rate tax (which has been incorporated into a bill introduced by Senator Dennis DeConcini) illustrate the range of options. The Bradley-Gephardt bill is a comprehensive income tax with moderately graduated rates; the Kemp-Kasten bill is a comprehensive income tax with one rate, which turns out on close examination to be a multiple-rate system; the Aaron-Galper plan is a comprehensive graduated consumption tax; and the Hall-Rabushka plan is a flat-rate wage and business income tax that is equivalent to a value-added tax. All the plans are intended to raise only enough revenue to replace the revenues from the present individual and corporation income taxes. To raise more revenues in order to reduce the deficit, higher rates would be needed.

The Bradley-Gephardt Bill

The Bradley-Gephardt plan would broaden the income tax base by treating capital gains as ordinary income, eliminating all the tax credits except the earned income credit for low-income workers, and repealing numerous tax preferences. Mortage interest would remain deductible, but all other interest would be deductible only to the extent of property income. (Any excess would be carried over to the following year.) No deduction would be allowed for two-earner couples, and special rates for heads of households would be eliminated. Deductions would still be allowed for state and local income and property taxes, charitable contributions, medical expenses, and casualty losses (each of the latter two limited to payments in excess of 10 percent of income), and mortgage interest. Personal exemptions would be increased to $1,600 for taxpayers and $1,000 for dependents, and the zero-bracket amount would be raised to $3,000 for single persons and $6,000 for married couples, which would lift the minimum taxable level for a family of four from $7,400 to $11,200.

The Bradley-Gephardt bill would replace the present individual income tax rate schedule with a flat normal tax and a graduated surtax, which would keep the distribution of tax burdens by income class about the same as it is today. The normal tax would be 14 percent and would apply to taxable income; that is, to adjusted gross income after deductions. The surtax would be 12 percent on income *before* deductions between $25,000 and $37,500 for single persons and $40,000 and $65,000 for married couples. For incomes above $37,500 and $65,000, the surtax rate would be 16 percent. Thus the tax rates would increase from 14 percent in the bottom bracket to 26 percent in the middle bracket and 30 percent in the top bracket. About 80 percent of all taxpayers would be subject only to the 14 percent rate.

The surtax is a controversial feature of the plan. Since no deductions are allowed in computing the amount of income subject to surtax, the value of the deductions that remain (for homeowners, charitable contributions, medical expenses, and casualty losses) as well as the personal exemptions would be limited to the normal tax, or 14 percent. For taxpayers in the top bracket, this would mean that more than half the remaining deductions (16 divided by 30) would in effect be eliminated.

The corporation income tax under the Bradley-Gephardt bill eliminates the lower rate on capital gains and other tax preferences, but the most important features of the bill are that the investment credit would be repealed and depreciation would be allowed for actual depreciation on the assumption that inflation averages about 6 percent a year. The tax rate on this broadened base would be a flat 30 percent, with no reduced rates for small corporations.

The Kemp-Kasten Bill

The Kemp-Kasten bill is similar in many respects to the Bradley-Gephardt plan, but there are differences both in the definition of income for tax purposes and in the tax rates. Kemp-Kasten provides full deductions for all interest payments, property taxes, and contributions, and for medical expenses in excess of 10 percent of income. Deductions for state and local income and sales taxes and for casualty losses are eliminated. Capital gains are adjusted for inflation, but for the first ten years taxpayers may choose to deduct 25 percent of net capital gains instead. Personal exemptions are raised from $1,000 to $2,000 per capita, and the zero-bracket amounts are increased from $2,300 to $2,700 for single persons and from $3,400 to $3,500 for joint returns. The higher exemptions and zero-bracket amounts are also adjusted for inflation. A special deduction is allowed under Kemp-Kasten for the first 20 percent of earnings up to the Social Security tax limit (almost $40,000 in 1985), and then it is phased down to zero at about $100,000.

The tax rate is set at 25 percent, which means that the rate on earned income after allowing for the special deduction would be reduced to 20 percent up to the Social Security limit. Above that limit, the deduction is phased down gradually until the 25 percent rate is reached above $100,000. The purpose of this provision is to keep the combined income and Social Security tax rate for most wage earners close to the present rate—11 percent or more for the income tax and 7.05 percent for Social Security.

The phase-down of the earnings deduction in effect increases the marginal tax rate to 28 percent. This means that, instead of one rate, the Kemp-Kasten bill actually proposes a 20 percent rate on earnings below $40,000, 28 percent on earnings between $40,000 and $100,000, 25 percent on earnings above $100,000 and on unearned incomes, and 18.75 percent on capital-gains receipts of those who prefer that rate to the inflation adjustment. Flat rates are not simple if they are accompanied by special deductions and exceptions.

Like the Bradley-Gephardt bill, the Kemp-Kasten bill would reduce the general corporation income tax rate from 46 percent to 30 percent, but there would be a special low rate of 15 percent on corporate income up to $50,000. The Kemp-Kasten bill would also eliminate the investment tax credit, but it would retain the present liberal depreciation allowances.

Congressman Jack Kemp and Senator Robert W. Kasten, Jr., believe that their plan would retain present average burdens for those with incomes up to $100,000, but it would reduce average tax rates above $100,000 by about 20 percent. Kemp argues that this revenue would be made up by the higher tax collections from the improved economic incentives, a claim that many question. Corporate tax collections would also be lower under the Kemp-Kasten bill than under the Bradley-Gephardt bill because of the differences in depreciation accounting under the two plans.

The Cash Flow Tax

Henry Aaron and Harvey Galper propose what they call a "lifetime" income tax. This is a graduated consumption or cash flow tax, with gifts and bequests included in the tax base. A tax on labor income and a consumption tax are equivalent if the taxpayers consume everything they earn during their lifetimes. The inclusion of gifts and bequests is needed to preserve the identity of the income and consumption taxes when viewed from a lifetime perspective.

In addition to the consumption tax, a net cash flow tax is substituted for the corporation income tax. The corporation tax base would include receipts from all sources other than the sale of stock, less business expenses, including investment. Receipts from borrowing would be included and debt-service payments would be deductible, but no deduction would be allowed for dividends paid to stockholders.

The tax rates on individuals would range from 5 percent to 32 percent, with an exemption of $11,250 for a family of four. The corporate tax would have a flat rate of 32 percent. These rates are predicated on the assumption that both taxes would be fully comprehensive. The present 10 percent deduction for two-earner couples would be continued, but all other personal deductions would be eliminated.

Aaron and Galper are quite sanguine about the possibility of limiting the lifetime exemption for gifts and bequests to $100,000 per person. The lifetime exemption under the present estate and gift tax will be $600,000 beginning in 1987. In addition, annual gifts of $10,000 per donee ($20,000 for a married couple) are excluded.

Even if Congress can be persuaded to lower the lifetime exemption, some annual exclusion will be needed simply to avoid the compliance headaches of keeping track of small gifts. Departures from comprehensiveness and failure to include gifts and bequests in the tax base would require increases in the tax rates and would also cut the link between the consumption tax and income tax on a lifetime basis.

A Simple Wage and Business Tax

Robert Hall and Alvin Rabushka propose the ultimate in flat taxes. They would tax labor income and pensions at the individual level and would have a separate tax on both corporate and noncorporate business. No deductions would be allowed under the wage tax, even for catastrophic medical expenses. The business tax would apply to total revenues of the enterprise less purchases of goods and services and compensation of employees. The personal exemption would begin at $12,600 for a family of four in 1985 prices and would be adjusted for inflation. The tax rate for both taxes is 19 percent. It can be shown that these taxes are exactly equivalent to a tax on total consumption in the economy or, what is equivalent, a value-added tax on consumer goods, both with a personal exemption.

Unlike the other tax plans, the Hall-Rabushka plan envisages repeal of the estate and gift taxes. They justify this drastic step on the ground that there is no place for a tax on wealth in a consumption tax system. They appear to be unconcerned about the social effects of the more concentrated distribution of wealth that would be generated by such a tax.

The Hall-Rabushka plan would result in a major redistribution of tax burdens from the rich to the poor and the middle-income classes. Assuming their estimate is correct—that only a 19 percent rate is needed to duplicate present revenues from the individual and corporation income taxes—the breaking point is in the neighborhood of $50,000. If a higher rate is needed, the breaking point would be higher. Like Kemp and Kasten, Hall and Rabushka believe that economic growth will make up the difference, but this is an optimistic assumption.

PROSPECTS FOR TAX REFORM

The idea of simplifying the income tax system and reducing the marginal tax rates is so appealing, one wonders why it was not implemented a long time ago. The reason is that the present complicated system grew up as a result of real pressures for tax preferences to which Congress felt obliged to respond. Moreover, not all the tax preferences are devices to permit the wealthy to escape taxation. Many of the most expensive deductions and exemptions benefit mainly the low- and middle-income classes (for example, homeowners, the aged, the unemployed), and few politicians care to risk the wrath of such large groups of voters.

If comprehensive taxation is to succeed, taxpayers will have to be persuaded that they will be better off with a broader tax base and lower tax rates. This argument will be difficult to "sell" because it must be acknowledged that some taxpayers—those who now benefit from the tax preferences—will be worse off. Only if the majority who will be better off demand tax reform will the politicians respond. The trouble is that the special-interest groups are well organized and do not hesitate to apply pressure on their congressmen and senators to defend their particular loopholes, or even to enlarge them.

The tax legislative process is not organized in a manner that will enhance the prospects for tax reforms. The two tax committees of Congress—the Ways and Means Committee and the Senate Finance Committee—consist of the most senior and most powerful members of Congress. They reached their positions by doing favors for important constituent groups, as well as by voting correctly on the big social, economic, and political issues. These groups are ever alert to defend the gains they have made, and attempts to eliminate these gains would risk political reprisals (through reduced contributions, public opposition to the incumbent's candidacy, and so on).

The legislative history of the income tax suggests that the prospects for tax reform are slim. Tax changes are usually incremental in nature, and a wholesale restructuring of the tax system in one grand bill does not seem to be in the cards. However, the current situation is different from what it has been in the past. The tax system has become too unfair, too complicated, and too costly to survive in its present form. Moreover, the large deficits now in prospect for years to come demand that action be taken to raise additional revenues. Such revenues will be obtained only if the tax system is perceived as fair and worthy of expansion. Comprehensive taxation provides the best prospect for reaching agreement on this difficult issue.

2 Broadening the Tax Base

The Staff of the
Joint Committee on Taxation

CHARACTERISTICS OF COMPREHENSIVE TAX PROPOSALS

While the details of recent comprehensive tax proposals vary substantially, it is useful to categorize into five groups the changes they would make in the present tax system:

1. The bills generally would expand the tax base by repealing a variety of deductions, exclusions, and credits in the present system.
2. Marginal tax rates applied to the base would be lowered substantially.
3. The degree of steepness in the rate schedule, the rate at which marginal tax rates increased with income, would be reduced.
4. The aggregate distribution of tax burdens by income class would be altered by some of the proposals.
5. The total amount of revenue raised by the corporate and individual income taxes would be changed by some of the proposals.

This chapter is based on the Joint Taxation Committee's *Analysis of Senate Proposals Relating to Comprehensive Tax Reform*, U.S. Congress, 6 August 1984, pp. 8–34.

This chapter considers some of the features of the present income tax which are relevant to these issues and contains a general discussion of them.

Changes in the Tax Base

All the proposals under discussion would make substantial changes in the tax base. In all cases, significant items not now subject to tax would be included in the base.

Many of the proposals adopt a relatively comprehensive definition of income as the primary basis for taxation. The designers of most of the proposals appear to have made the judgment that income is the best measure of taxpaying capacity and that taxpayers with equal income should have equal tax liability. In addition, it appears that they believe that many of the exclusions, deductions, and credits in the present system are inequitable, inefficient, or complex, or at least they have decided that the benefits these provisions may have are outweighed by the advantages of the other changes made by the bills, such as reductions in marginal tax rates.

Lowering Marginal Tax Rates

In all of the proposals, marginal tax rates are substantially reduced. This reduction appears to be motivated by efficiency and equity considerations.

Efficiency

Many economists would agree that high marginal taxes can cause considerable economic inefficiency, both by interfering with the incentives for work and saving, and by magnifying the effects caused by differences between the tax base that may be chosen purely for efficiency reasons and the base that actually is implemented in the law.

An individual's marginal tax rate is the rate applicable to the last or to the next dollar of income received. If an individual is subject to a 25-percent marginal rate, then the return to additional work effort and saving is reduced by 25 percent. For example, if this individual works on an overtime assignment that pays $40, the after-tax reward to this work effort would be $30. A higher marginal tax rate would reduce the return to this work effort even further, affecting the incentive to undertake the assignment. A similar point may be made with respect to investment decisions. If the individual with a 25 percent marginal rate invests in a security with a 10 percent return, the after-tax return would be 7.5 percent. Thus the marginal tax rate affects the incentive to save rather than use the same resources for current consumption. The same reasoning may be used to show that marginal tax rates also influence the incentives to engage in activities that are heavily taxed versus those that are lightly taxed. With high marginal rates, for example, there is more incentive to invest in lightly taxed investments or to take jobs in which a high proportion of compensation is in the form of nontaxable fringe benefits than would be the case with low marginal rates.

Effect on Labor Supply

The effect of changes in marginal tax rates in distorting incentives is sometimes referred to as the "substitution effect." Most of the studies that have been performed on the effect of after-tax wage rates on work effort have found that the substitution effect of after-tax wage changes in hours worked is quite small for husbands but rather large for wives, especially wives with children. Since the substitution effect is measured by holding after-tax income constant, it is the proper measure of the incentive effect of a marginal rate reduction, as opposed to the "income" effect that would occur because of the income increase attributable to any tax reduction. This empirical finding is confirmed in one of the more recent and sophisticated studies,[1] except that a significant substitution effect is found for husbands, as well as wives. Thus these studies indicate that if marginal tax rates were lowered, holding other factors (including after-tax income) constant, some individuals would be willing to work a larger number of hours. This could be manifested as greater willingness to work full-time instead of part-time, greater acceptance of overtime assignments, less absenteeism, and a larger number of individuals in the labor force.[2]

It should also be noted that there are several other possible effects of marginal tax rates on work-related activities. First, it has been argued that reduction in marginal tax rates could improve compliance with the income tax, although there is little evidence that bears directly on this question. Second, it has been argued that high marginal tax rates have induced employees to demand a larger portion of their compensation in the form of tax-free fringe benefits, such as health insurance, than would be the case with lower marginal rates, and this substitution of fringe benefits for cash may reduce the efficiency with which the economy satisfies employees' needs. To the extent that such effects exist, they would be lessened if marginal tax rates were lowered.

Effect of Marginal Tax Rates on Saving

If an individual saves a dollar rather than spending it on current consumption, he or she generally will be able to have in excess of one dollar available for consumption in a future period. The amount of this excess depends on the return available for funds saved and on the marginal tax rate applicable to this return. The quantity of consumer goods that can be purchased in the future with a given amount of money will depend on the rate of inflation. Thus, the after-tax return (adjusted for inflation) determines the extra future consumption that a person can have by saving and thus sacrificing one dollar of current consumption. The lower the after-tax return, the more attractive is the option to consume now rather than save. As an important determinant of the after-tax return, the marginal tax rate is likely to affect this choice.

As in the analysis of work effort, it is important to distinguish between the income and substitution effects of marginal tax-rate changes on the choice between current and future consumption. Any tax reduction, including a reduction in marginal rates, will increase after-tax income and thus generally will lead to an increase in both current and future consumption. However, marginal tax-rate reductions also would have incentive, or substitution effects, because they change the rate at which the taxpayer can trade off between current and future consumption. This discussion emphasizes the substitution effects, which are unique to marginal tax-rate reductions and which measure the economic inefficiency created by taxes.

Three distinct sources of concern with high marginal tax rates have been cited by economists who have analyzed the effects of the income tax on current and future consumption. The first concern is the effect of the marginal tax rates on individuals' incentives to consume in current rather than future periods; the second is the effect of marginal tax rates on aggregate saving, investment, and productivity; and the third involves the effect of the tax system on the composition of saving as a result of its effect on incentives to invest in lightly taxed versus heavily taxed activities and its incentive to borrow—the deduction for nonbusiness interest.

The fact that the marginal tax rates implicit in the current income tax discourage future consumption creates a distortion (relative to a tax system with a marginal rate of zero, such as a per capita head tax). The importance of this distortion depends on the responsiveness of future consumption to a change in the after-tax rate of return on saving, holding income constant. Empirical studies of this sensitivity are much less numerous than those of labor-supply response. The methodological difficulties of studying the responsiveness of consumption to the rate of return are greater because the expected real return (net of expected inflation) must be measured and because the statistical analysis must be performed using time series of observations on total U.S. income and consumption. This methodology requires the assumption that the quantitative relationships among the variables have been unchanged for a long period of time. In spite of these methodological problems, empirical studies do indicate that individuals' plans for future consumption are sensitive to the after-tax rate of return. The marginal tax rate on capital income also may affect the choice between labor and leisure, as well as the choice between present and future consumption. For example, a greater after-tax rate of return may make it more attractive for individuals to work for the purpose of increasing their consumption in retirement years. However, this sort of effect has not been firmly substantiated in empirical research.

The second major concern that has been raised concerning the effect of marginal tax rates on capital income has been their effect on aggregate savings and, thus, investment and productivity. For a variety of reasons, however, the link between aggregate investment and the marginal tax rates in the individual income tax is very uncertain. First, investment may be affected much more directly by other factors, such as the tax treatment of depreciation allowances. Second, the effect of income tax changes on private saving could be offset to the extent that there is a revenue loss, which leads to less government saving. Finally, even though it is likely that a higher after-tax return may increase future consumption, it is not clear as a theoretical matter that personal savings would increase simultaneously. This is the case because a higher return on savings actually lowers the amount that an individual needs to save in the current period in order to achieve any future consumption goal. Personal saving would increase in response to an increase in the after-tax rate of return only if desired future consumption increases sufficiently to offset this effect. Whether this is in fact the case can be determined only by empirical studies. Although these studies are extremely difficult to perform, there is some indication that future consumption may be stimulated sufficiently by increasing the after-tax return that total personal saving may increase modestly in response to such a change.

The income tax also influences decisions about the particular forms in which taxpayers do their saving, which affects the allocation of capital in the economy. The first concern is that the income tax imposes heavier tax rates on some activities than others (such as tax shelters, owner-occupied housing, and precious metals). This provides an incentive to shift from heavily taxed activities, which may be more productive, to lightly taxed activities. The size of this incentive depends on the marginal tax rate. Thus it is argued that reducing the marginal tax rate may encourage individuals to shift from less productive to more productive forms of saving. The second concern relates to the present-law deduction for nonbusiness interest. Since this provision is in effect an encouragement for borrowing—that is, dissaving—it is argued that reducing marginal tax rates could encourage saving by reducing the incentive to borrow. Finally, it is argued that because the income from assets subject to capital gains treatment is taxed only when the assets are sold, high marginal tax rates discourage sales and prevent these assets from being employed in their most efficient uses. Thus lower marginal income tax rates could increase efficiency by reducing this "lock-in" effect.

The bills discussed here take several approaches to improving saving incentives. All of the bills attempt to achieve greater uniformity in the tax treatment of saving and income from capital by reducing or eliminating preferential treatment for certain types of saving relative to others. Also, the bills reduce marginal tax rates, which reduces the adverse impact of whatever distortions remain. Some of the bills, however, go farther than this and attempt to structure a system in which the effective tax rate on saving is zero.

Equity

From an equity perspective, reducing marginal tax rates also may be viewed as desirable. Many argue that it is unfair for a high portion of each additional dollar of income earned by an individual to be absorbed as increased tax liability. In passing the Economic Recovery Tax Act of 1981, Congress lowered the highest marginal rate in the tax schedules from 70 percent to 50 percent. Much of the discussion of this change involved the belief that a marginal tax rate as high as 70 percent caused undue interference with the incentives for efficient economic performance. However, another important source of support for this reduction was the feeling that it was unfair for the tax system to claim more than half of each additional dollar earned by taxpayers. Presumably, this indicates that one accepted equity objective of tax policy is to keep marginal tax rates below some threshold level.

Reducing the Progressivity of the Rate Schedules

The authors of the proposals appear to believe that it is desirable to reduce significantly the number of tax brackets in the rate schedules and to reduce the difference between the bottom and top rates of the income tax. Some of the proposals have one flat tax rate that applies to all income not exempt from taxation.

It is important to emphasize that the issue of the degree of progressivity in the rate schedules is to some extent independent of the broad vertical equity issue of the relative distribution of tax burdens by income class. That is, the distribution of tax burdens is affected not only by the degree of progressivity in the rate schedules, but by other structural elements of the income tax as well. For example, during 1981 the Ways and Means Committee considered a proposal to reduce the number of brackets in the rate schedule, to widen the first bracket so that a majority of taxpayers were subject to the same tax rate, and to increase the personal exemption and zero bracket amount to offset the rate increases imposed on the lowest income taxpayers. These revised rate schedules produced approximately the same amount of progressivity as under prior law. Thus, some flattening of the rate schedule is possible even without large changes in the distribution of the tax burden.

There are several advantages to a flat or flattened rate schedule. For example, if taxpayers are more likely to be in the same tax bracket over a period of years, tax considerations would be less likely to influence the timing of transactions. This would reduce one of the sources of inefficiency of a progressive rate schedule. If most taxpayers faced the same tax rate, there would be less incentive to shift income to low-bracket family members, which may improve the perception of equity in the system. The difference in tax treatment between married couples and single individuals would be reduced, since, in a system in which married couples may pool their income and file a joint return, this difference arises from the fact that the amount of income taxed at each rate depends on marital status. Finally, a flatter tax rate would allow a closer correspondence between amounts withheld and tax liability. In a system in which the tax rate did not depend on taxpayer's income, as is the case under the present Social Security payroll tax, withholding could be closer to tax liability in the vast majority of cases.[3] It should be emphasized that although some flattening is compatible with a progressive distribution of tax burdens—that is, a system in which tax liability as a percentage of income increases as income rises—adopting a rate schedule with just one rate would impose strict limits on the degree of progressivity that could be obtained. Some progressivity could be attained by exempting some fixed amount of income from taxation for all individuals, but the pattern of progressivity in the present system probably could not be duplicated.

Changing the Distribution of Tax Burdens by Income Class

The present individual income tax system exhibits a substantial degree of progressivity. The average tax rate rises from a negative figure in the bottom class (owing to the refundable earned income tax credit) to about 25 percent in the highest class. The rate in the highest income class is approximately double the average tax rate.

Choosing a pattern of distribution by income class depends primarily on vertical equity considerations. As noted before, this is largely a matter of value judgment. Some argue that the present distribution pattern should be preserved in any alternative proposal, while others may believe that the present distribution is either too progressive or not progressive enough. In addition, efficiency may be a consideration in the selection of the distribution of tax burdens because the relatively high marginal tax rates on higher income taxpayers necessary to achieve the desired distribution may result in a significant increase in the inefficiency caused by the system.

Achieving Specified Revenue Targets

One of the key decisions that must be made in analyzing or designing a comprehensive tax proposal is the choice of a revenue target. Clearly, if there is substantial base broadening with no changes in marginal tax rates, total revenue will be increased, and if marginal tax rates are lowered without changing the tax base, total revenue will be reduced. Several of the proposals appear to be designed so that the new combination of tax rates and tax base would produce approximately the same revenue as is expected under present law for a chosen fiscal year. However, if a judgment is made that this level is either too low or too high, base-broadening and tax-rate decisions can be adjusted accordingly.

Conclusion

Each of the comprehensive tax proposals under discussion would make changes in at least several of the five areas discussed here. It certainly would be possible to achieve base broadening by itself, although this would change the total revenue raised and the pattern of distribution by income class. Similarly, a proposal could be designed to reduce progressivity in the rate schedules while leaving the tax base, the distribution by income class, and total revenue unchanged. Marginal rates could be reduced or increased, making no changes in the tax base, but total revenue obviously would change. Even though the five areas may be logically distinct, substantial change in any one appears to bring into consideration other objectives. The balance among these objectives depends on the equity, efficiency, simplicity, and other tax-policy considerations.

ISSUES IN DESIGNING THE TAX BASE

One definition of a person's income is the amount he could potentially consume over a period of time without reducing his wealth. Under this definition, income during a year would equal the person's actual consumption in the year plus the increase in his wealth (his savings) between the beginning and the end of the year. This, in turn, would equal the sum of wages, interest, dividends, and other receipts, minus costs incurred in earning income, plus any appreciation, realized or unrealized, in the value of the person's wealth.

The present income tax base differs from this theoretical "accretion" concept of income in a number of respects. These can be divided into ways in which the basic tax structure fails to correspond to a pure income tax (structural tax issues) and specific tax provisions that are intended to provide incentives for taxpayers to engage in particular activities or to provide relief for particular types of taxpayers (tax expenditures).

Structural Tax Issues

There are five principal structural tax issues:

1. The definition of income from capital and the treatment of borrowing during periods of inflation.
2. The taxation of corporate-source income.
3. The treatment of noncash income.
4. The treatment of unrealized income.
5. The treatment of savings, and whether a tax on consumer expenditures would be more appropriate than an income tax.

Indexing the Definition of Income for Inflation

Inflation creates a problem for an income tax because it increases the difficulty of defining taxable income from capital and of properly treating borrowing. A proper definition is necessary if ability to pay is judged to be measured by income and if efficiency considerations call for equal tax rates on income from various activities. This problem is most easily seen by considering a case in which a person buys an asset for $50,000, holds it for a period during which the general price level doubles, and sells that asset for $100,000. In reality, the taxpayer has experienced no real increase in his wealth and has no income from the sale of the asset; the purchasing power sacrificed in order to buy the asset is exactly equal to the purchasing power represented by the sale of the asset. However, under present law, the taxpayer must report a long-term capital gain of $50,000 of which 40 percent is included in adjusted gross income.

A similar problem arises in measuring depreciation. In theory, depreciation should be a measure of the real loss of value of an asset during a time period. If a taxpayer buys a building for $50,000, he is presently able to claim cost-recovery deductions amounting to $50,000 over an eighteen-year period. However, if rapid inflation occurs during that period, the purchasing power represented by the cumulative cost-recovery deductions will be less than that sacrificed to purchase the building, and real income will not be measured exactly. The same problem arises in inventory accounting when businesses use the first-in, first-out (FIFO) method of accounting in periods of inflation, since increases in the value of inventory from inflation are treated as taxable income even though the increase does not result in any real increase in asset values.

The treatment of debt in periods of inflation also fails to conform to an exact measure of real income. Inflation enables the borrower to repay debt with less valuable dollars, which represents income to the borrower that currently goes untaxed. To the extent that interest payments rise to compensate for anticipated inflation, the additional interest is deductible. Conversely, the erosion of the real value of indebtedness is a cost to the lender that he is currently unable to deduct, even though any additional interest to compensate for inflation is included in taxable income.

It should be noted that the issues discussed here relating to the definition of the income tax base are entirely separate from the effect of inflation in narrowing the real width of the tax brackets and reducing the real value of the personal exemption and the other fixed-dollar amounts used to determine tax liability (so-called bracket creep). For the individual income tax for years after 1984, bracket creep was largely eliminated by the indexing provisions of the Economic Recovery Tax Act of 1981.

One way to deal with these definitional problems would be to enact a more comprehensive indexing program in which the definition of income from capital and the treatment of debt would be adjusted for inflation so as to achieve an accurate measure of real income. This would involve four specific changes: (1) indexing the basis of assets by the rate of inflation for purposes both of computing gain or loss on the sale or exchange of those assets and of computing depreciation, depletion, and other capital-cost-recovery deductions, (2) adopting a new system of inventory accounting in which costs would be indexed for inflation, (3) requiring borrowers to include in taxable income the gain that results when inflation erodes the real value of their debt, and (4) allowing lenders to deduct the loss that results when inflation erodes the real value of debt.

While the tax-writing committees have never considered such a complete indexing program, there has been serious consideration of some of its elements. In its version of the Revenue Act of 1978, the House passed an indexing adjustment to basis for capital gains and losses on corporate stock, real estate, and tangible personal property. In its version of the Tax Equity and Fiscal Responsibility Act of 1982, the Senate passed a similar provision for corporate stock and real estate. Indexing basis for purposes of computing depreciation deductions was discussed in the context of depreciation reform in 1980 and 1981.

There is little disagreement that a comprehensive income tax would not reach an accurate definition of income without indexing. However, more comprehensive, exact indexing would add a good deal of complexity to the tax system, particularly the exact indexing adjustments for inventory accounting, borrowing, and lending. Even a program of partial indexing, limited to capital cost recovery and measurement of gain and loss, would add some complexity, which might not be worth the effort at sufficiently low rates of inflation.

In place of indexing the definition of income, Congress has adopted several ad hoc approaches to alleviating the distortions created by inflation. The last-in, first-out (LIFO) method of inventory accounting is, in most cases, an adequate substitute for a more complicated indexed system. The exclusion for 60 percent of long-term capital gains and the ACRS method of recovering the costs of equipment and structures were both motivated in some degree by a desire to offset some of the distortions in income measurement caused by inflation. Furthermore, the distortion caused by the failure of the present system to make inflation adjustments for debt is reduced by the fact that the adjustments made by the borrower and lender would, to some extent, offset each other (and would be completely offsetting if the two had identical marginal tax rates).

These ad hoc provisions, however, are themselves deviations from what would be appropriate in a comprehensive income tax and create some inequities and distortions that to a degree offset the benefits they provide in reducing the distortions created by inflation. For example, an ad hoc adjustment such as ACRS or the 60 percent capital-gains deduction will only be accurate at a single rate of inflation, and actual inflation rates are likely to be different. The present rate of inflation, for example, is significantly lower than the inflation rate at the time both the 60 percent capital gains deduction and ACRS were enacted.

Thus there is no entirely satisfactory solution to the problem of properly defining the tax base in periods of inflation. Any solution involves trade-offs between complexity, equity, and various kinds of distortions.

Taxation of Corporate Income

Corporate integration. Under present law, corporate-source income is taxed at the corporate level under the corporate income tax. In addition, dividend distributions are taxed under the individual income tax, and increases in the value of corporate stock that result from earnings retention are taxed as capital gains to the shareholder. Clearly, this system does violence to the principle that all income be taxed alike. Dividends may be subject to a combined corporate and individual tax burden as high as 73 percent.[4] Retained earnings bear a 46 percent corporate tax plus a capital-gains tax when the shareholder sells his stock. Corporate-source income, therefore, will generally be taxed at the same marginal tax rate as other kinds of income only in the case of corporations with zero marginal tax rates (that is, negative taxable income or excess credits) who pay out all their earnings as dividends. In other cases, corporate-source income will be taxed more or less heavily than the shareholder's ordinary income.

The present system is held responsible for creating economic inefficiency by distorting several types of business decisions. Shareholders have an incentive to invest in assets other than corporate stock in order to avoid double taxation. Corporations have an incentive to finance their operations with debt rather than equity because interest payments are deductible (and hence not subject to double taxation). Corporations also have an incentive to retain earnings, rather than pay out dividends, to avoid double taxation if they can ultimately distribute that money to shareholders as part of a liquidation, through repurchase of their own shares, or in connection with a takeover, the proceeds from which are usually subject to tax at capital-gains rates. These distortions caused by the present system of taxing corporations have been blamed for reducing capital formation and productivity growth, preventing the allocation of capital to its most efficient uses, weakening the nation's financial structure through excessive reliance on debt, and encouraging mergers and acquisitions.

One way to treat corporate-source income would be to tax all of it—dividends and retained earnings—as if it were earned directly by shareholders. This is essentially the way subchapter S corporations are treated today. The corporate income tax could be retained as a withholding tax, for which shareholders would receive a refundable credit on their own tax returns just as they do for the present withholding taxes on wages.

Unfortunately, when applied to large corporations with complex structures, this type of complete integration of the corporate and individual income taxes presents serious technical problems.[5] As a result, much more attention has focused on simply reducing or eliminating the double taxation of dividends, without modifying the treatment of retained earnings. This can be done either through the dividend-deduction approach or the shareholder-credit approach.

The dividend-deduction approach is the simplest way to eliminate double taxation of dividends. Corporations simply would deduct their dividends paid in determining taxable income, in effect exempting from the corporate income tax whatever income is distributed as dividends, leaving that income to be taxed once at the shareholder level.

Under the shareholder-credit approach, a shareholder would make two adjustments. First, he would "gross-up" the amount of the dividend included in gross income by the amount of the corporate tax deemed paid with respect to that income. Second, he would claim a refundable tax credit for the amount of the gross-up. If the shareholder credits with respect to a corporation's dividends exceeded the amount of corporate tax actually paid by the corporation, it would have to pay an additional tax to make up the shortfall.[6]

A number of considerations are relevant in choosing between these two approaches. The dividends-paid deduction is simpler. However, the shareholder credit provides flexibility under which, for example, the credit can be denied to tax-exempt organizations and foreign shareholders for whom there is no U.S. double taxation. This would reduce the revenue impact.

The argument for relieving the double taxation of dividends is stronger to the extent that the corporate income tax base is broadened. One problem that arises with the present relatively narrow corporate tax base is that many profitable companies have zero or low marginal tax rates because they use tax preferences, while others have substantial tax liability and are subject to the top 46-percent marginal tax rate. These differences create inequities and distortions between firms, and these would be exacerbated if a new deduction for dividends paid or shareholder credit were added to the system. On the other hand, the argument for relieving the double taxation of dividends is weaker to the extent that marginal tax rates in the individual and corporate income taxes are reduced from their present levels, since the size of the distortions caused by double taxation is directly related to these marginal rates. In addition, eliminating double taxation would narrow the tax base and thus preclude further opportunities for reducing marginal rates.

Consistent Treatment of Corporations and Individuals

Another structural issue is the extent to which there should be consistency between the corporate and individual income taxes, both in terms of the tax bases and the tax rates. For example, if certain tax benefits are provided to corporations and not individuals, there may be an incentive to conduct business in the corporate form, and there may be inequities and competitive advantages in favor of corporate business. Also, if the corporate tax rate exceeds the top individual tax rate and there is no double taxation of dividends, corporations will have an incentive to pay out earnings as dividends up to the point where their dividends-paid deduction exhausts their taxable income. This would represent a significant change in the pattern of corporate finance.

Deferral of Tax on Earnings of Foreign Corporations

Under current law, United States persons who invest directly in foreign countries are subject to current U.S. tax on their foreign income (subject to a foreign tax credit that may offset U.S. tax on that foreign income). U.S. persons who invest in foreign countries through foreign subsidiary corporations generally may defer tax on the undistributed earnings of the subsidiaries until repatriation. Although Congress has enacted exceptions to this general rule,[7] if a controlled foreign corporation's earnings do not arise from certain designated activities, its U.S. shareholders are not currently taxable on the foreign corporation's earnings, but instead defer tax (subject to a foreign tax credit) until distribution of the earnings.

A foreign tax credit in general is intended to follow the principle of capital export neutrality—that domestic and foreign investments receive the same U.S. tax treatment. It has been argued that the current system of deferral of the undistributed earnings of U.S.-owned foreign corporations does not comport with that principle, however. By allowing U.S. companies to operate currently in foreign countries under local tax rules rather than U.S. tax rules, deferral can create a U.S. tax preference for foreign investment over U.S. investment in cases where local rules produce the smaller tax. If current investment incentives were reduced in conjunction with a major revision of the U.S. income tax, the significance of this preference would be increased.

Some have argued that repeal of deferral could simplify rules governing the treatment of foreign income and could reduce or eliminate a variety of tax-planning opportunities that arise upon the interposition of a foreign corporation between the taxpayer and foreign-source income. These include (1) the ability to manipulate the foreign tax credit that arises when taxpayers conduct some foreign operations directly and other foreign operations through foreign subsidiaries, (2) the opportunity for U.S. taxpayers to decide when certain income will become subject to U.S. tax, and (3) the incentive for U.S. taxpayers to avoid U.S. tax by undercharging foreign subsidiaries for goods or services.

However, others contend that repeal of deferral could discourage exports, because some foreign subsidiaries of U.S. persons sell U.S. goods abroad and benefit from deferral. Repeal could engender a significant audit burden on the Internal Revenue Service and would result in unfavorable reactions by foreign countries where U.S. persons form foreign subsidiaries.

Noncash Income

Income that is received in a form other than cash often presents problems in an income tax, particularly when the cash value of the income is hard to determine. The principal types of noncash income include fringe benefits and imputed rent on owner-occupied homes and consumer durables.

Fringe benefits. Present law excludes certain statutory fringe benefits from gross income and, generally beginning in 1985, taxes all other fringe benefits at the excess of their fair market value over any amounts paid by the employee for the benefits.[8] In most cases, the statutory fringes were intended by Congress as tax incentives for employers to provide compensation in particular ways, and some of the statutory provisions contain restrictions designed to carry out Congress' intent that these fringe benefits should be widely available (such as coverage requirements for qualified pension plans). In other cases, the statutory fringes were intended to codify established practices where business reasons, other than simply providing compensation, were adduced for employers to encourage employees to use the products they sell.

Under the bills discussed here, the tax base would be broadened by repealing some of the present exclusions for fringe benefits. These benefits may be difficult to tax in certain situations. Issues that are often encountered with respect to fringe benefits include the valuation of the benefit (on the basis, for example, of fair market value or employer's cost), the allocation to individuals of benefits made available to employees as a group,[9] and consistent treatment of one large benefit with various smaller benefits that aggregate to the same value but involve much more effort to account for. In selecting the treatment of fringe benefits, the problems of inexact and complex valuations would have to be balanced against the equity and efficiency advantages of a broader tax base.

Imputed income. The two principal types of imputed income are rent on owner-occupied homes and consumer durables. It has been argued that a homeowner, under a pure income tax, would be treated as someone in the business of renting his house. He would report as income the fair market rental on the house (imputed rent) and deduct all the costs associated with the house, including interest, taxes, utilities, and depreciation. Under present law, imputed rent is not taxed, deductions are allowed for interest and taxes, and deductions are denied for utilities, depreciation, and most other costs associated with homeownership. Thus the tax preference for homeownership equals the imputed rent minus the nondeductible costs.[10] Consumer durables are treated the same way: No imputed rent is included, but a deduction is allowed for "consumer" interest and taxes.

Few people seriously propose taxing imputed rent on owner-occupied homes or consumer durables because valuing the rentals would be extremely complicated and there is a public policy to encourage homeownership.[11] Rather, proposals to scale back the homeowner and consumer durable preferences generally take the form of limits on, or repeal of, the mortgage or consumer interest and property tax deductions. However, these proposals are not entirely free from problems of their own. Unless it were accompanied by repeal of the deduction for other nonbusiness taxes, repeal of the property tax deduction could be viewed as discriminating against those states and localities that rely disproportionately on the property tax. Limits on, or repeal of, the mortgage and consumer interest deductions tend to cut back the preference in proportion to the extent that the taxpayer finances his home or durables with debt rather than equity, and such a nonuniform scaling back of preferences may make the system less, rather than more, equitable. Furthermore, there is a practical problem that money is fungible and that there is no real economic distinction between mortgage and consumer interest, on the one hand, and other kinds of interest that are legitimate deductions in a tax on net income, on the other. However, the tax system has traditionally made a distinction between personal and business expenditures.

These types of considerations lead to other proposals for reducing the distortions and inequities associated with the treatment of interest and homeownership. For example, it has been suggested that all interest deductions be limited to investment income. None of the bills attempts to tax imputed rent on homes or durables; however, several repeal or limit interest and tax deductions.

Unrealized Income

Some types of income consist of increases in the value of assets prior to the time when the taxpayer actually receives the income, such as by selling or exchanging the assets. Taxing such unrealized income would present two problems: (1) in some cases, it may be difficult to value the asset in order to measure the income properly; and (2) the taxpayer may not have access to cash with which to pay his tax.

Capital gains and losses is the area where unrealized income creates the most serious problems. Assuming that taxing gains and deducting losses as they accrue is ruled out because of the valuation and liquidity problems,[12] the only alternative is to tax them when realized; that is, when the asset is sold or exchanged or some other recognition event occurs. Because selling an asset is generally within the taxpayer's discretion, a tax on realized gains gives taxpayers an incentive to defer realization in order to postpone the tax.[13] This, in turn, has been a justification for providing preferential treatment for long-term capital gains, the argument being that full taxation of such gains at high ordinary rates would discourage sales of appreciated property to such an extent that it would be counterproductive. Moreover, the fact that realization of gains and losses is discretionary has been the justification for imposing ad hoc limits on the deductibility of capital losses.[14] Without such limits, taxpayers who own a variety of assets could realize their losses and defer their gains, thereby escaping tax despite the fact that they had substantial real income. Thus the treatment of capital gains deviates in a number of respects from what would exist in a pure income tax.

In recent years Congress has moved toward taxing some unrealized income, generally in areas where the valuation and liquidity problems were not significant, the income tended to be received by sophisticated taxpayers, and there was serious potential for tax avoidance. In 1969 Congress required periodic inclusions of discount income on corporate original-issue discount bonds.[15] In 1981 Congress adopted a mark-to-market system of accrual taxation for commodity futures contracts, and in 1984 it extended that system to many options transactions.

Tax Treatment of Saving and Consumption Taxes

A number of analysts believe that the individual income tax should be replaced by a tax on consumer spending, so that the types of savings currently in the tax base would be exempt. In general, their analysis is that national welfare would be increased if greater savings could be funneled into greater investment that ultimately leads to higher levels of production. Two taxes that have been discussed in this regard are the consumed income tax and the value-added tax.

Individuals would continue to be the tax filing units under a consumed income tax. It would not be necessary for taxpayers to add up all their purchases of consumer goods and services. Rather, a consumption tax could be implemented through several modifications of the income tax, which make use of the arithmetical result that a person's after-tax income is either spent on consumption or saved. Thus a consumption tax base could be implemented by starting with an income tax base, allowing taxpayers to deduct all purchases of assets during the year, all tax payments, and all repayment of debt, and requiring them to add to the tax base the proceeds from all sales of assets and from all borrowing. A graduated rate structure could be applied to this base to produce a progressive tax, like the current income tax. Moreover, because a consumed income tax, like the current income tax, would be a personal tax, any additional personal circumstances (such as family size) that may be deemed relevant to equitable taxation could be taken into account. Although there is a history of academic analysis of the consumed income tax, it appears that only India and Sri Lanka have had experience with implementing it. Both countries have since repealed their consumed income tax.

Businesses would be the tax filing unit under a value-added tax. The value added by a business, and the base of the consumption-type value-added tax, is the difference between its sales proceeds and the cost of raw materials, semifinished goods, capital goods, and other items that it has purchased from other businesses. Thus if a business has sales of $100 and purchases $80 of goods and services from other businesses, its value added is $20. This will equal the sum of the wages and salaries it pays for the use of labor, the interest it pays for the use of capital, and its profits. Under one method of tax computation, the business would apply the tax rate to this base and remit the tax. Under an alternative method, generally used in Europe, the business would compute a tentative tax on sales proceeds and a tentative tax credit for purchases from other businesses and then remit the difference. Since the value-added tax on all sales to other businesses would be offset by subsequent tax credits, the only value-added tax that matters from the standpoint of overall revenues is the tax collected at the retail level, where there is no offsetting credit. (Thus, some argue, a third alternative would simply be to impose a national retail sales tax.) Exporters would claim a rebate for the value-added tax they paid when they acquired the goods for export, and importers would pay tax on the value of imported goods.

Conceptually, there are several types of value-added taxes, differentiated by their treatment of the cost of capital goods. The consumption-type of value-added tax is generally in use in European countries, where standard tax rates cluster between 15 and 20 percent. In many countries, exemptions or reduced tax rates are provided for numerous items—food, housing rent, medical services, water, and newspapers are examples—while tax rates above the standard tax rate may apply to luxury items. In many cases, these value-added taxes succeeded other consumption taxes, such as a turnover tax on all sales, a manufacturers' sales tax, a wholesalers' sales tax, or a retail sales tax. The turnover tax has been criticized for effectively imposing a higher tax on value added early in the production and distribution process (because it is taxable again in later stages), thus providing incentives for businesses to integrate vertically. A manufacturers' or wholesalers' sales tax would alleviate this problem because they are single-stage taxes; however, by failing to tax value added at the retail stage, such taxes create distortions against products where little value added occurs at the retail level.

Consumption taxes may be levied on a more limited basis for the purposes of raising revenue, discouraging consumption of specific products, or financing public expenditures closely related to the consumption of specific products. For example, the United States currently imposes taxes on the consumption of communications services, alcoholic beverages, cigarettes, and highway motor fuels. A proposal to tax energy consumption has also been considered.

Effect on incentives. Proponents of the consumption tax base argue that the income tax, by taxing income from capital, encourages taxpayers to consume their income now rather than save for future consumption and that a consumption tax would not distort this decision. Advocates of the income tax do not generally dispute this proposition but argue that the effect is not large enough to justify a change, that society can increase its saving by reducing government budget deficits, that other economic inefficiencies would be caused by the high marginal tax rates that would be necessary if saving were excluded from the tax base, and that, in any event, the emphasis on savings (rather than consumption) as the key to economic growth is misplaced.

Equity. Advocates of the consumption tax also argue that such a tax would be more equitable. Consider a simple example in which two taxpayers each earn $100. One consumes his after-tax income immediately, while the other invests it at 10 percent and consumes the proceeds the next year. Under an income tax with a 50-percent rate, both taxpayers would pay $50 in the first year, but the saver would pay an additional $2.50 on his $5 in the second year. Under a consumption tax, the taxpayer who spends in the first year would pay $50 that year, while the saver would pay $55 in the second year; that is, the present value of their tax burden would be the same. (Under an income tax limited to personal service income, they both would pay $50 in the first year, so their tax burdens would be identical in both years.) Proponents of a consumption tax argue that these two taxpayers are similarly situated because they have exactly the same opportunities over the two-year period and that it is equitable for them to pay the same tax either directly (as in an income tax on personal service income) or in present-value terms (as in a consumption tax).

Critics of the consumption-tax approach argue that a year-by-year comparison is more appropriate than a lifetime perspective, and that, from this standpoint, the two taxpayers are only similarly situated in the first year, with the saver better off in the second year and hence able to pay more tax that year. They also argue that the equity argument in favor of the consumption tax hinges on treating bequests as consumption and taxing them as such when a person dies. This, however, would be a controversial aspect of any consumption tax, since the bequests would be taxed again when consumed by the heirs. Moreover, taxpayers who are consuming more than their income because they are facing hard times, like the unemployed, would fare worse under a consumption tax than under an income tax, which may not be considered a fair result. Other taxpayers whose burdens would be higher under a consumption tax would include the elderly and parents putting their children through college. Perhaps most fundamentally, critics doubt that vertical equity in the distribution of tax burdens, gauged relative to the ability to pay taxes, can be achieved under a consumption tax.

Problems with the income tax. One argument for a consumption tax is that it would moot many of the questions that make it difficult to structure an income tax. A consumption tax would require no special rules for indexing the definition of income from capital and borrowing for inflation, capital gains and losses, depreciation, inventory accounting, or unrealized income. However, some structural problems with the income tax, like the treatment of many fringe benefits and of imputed income, would remain. Moreover, a consumption tax could create some new problems, like the treatment of gifts and bequests and the multitude of distinctions necessary to implement any exemptions or differential tax rates (as between necessities and luxuries, for example), that may be deemed necessary for furthering equity goals or other social considerations.

Marginal tax rates. A consumption base would be narrower than a comprehensive income base (although not necessarily narrower than the present income tax base), and higher-income people tend to save a larger percentage of their income than others. Therefore, to raise a given amount of revenue with a given degree of progressivity, the consumption base would require higher marginal tax rates than an income base. These higher rates would increase the ill effects of whatever distortions remained in the consumption tax system.

Transition issues. There would be difficulties in effecting a transition from an income tax to a consumption tax. It would be unfair, for example, to tax consumption from wealth that had been accumulated from after-tax income under the prior income tax. A transition rule to prevent such double taxation, however, such as allowing taxpayers to deduct the basis of assets held on the effective date of the consumption tax in order to grandfather consumption out of previously taxed income, would have a large revenue loss in the early years of the tax and would virtually exempt many wealthy people from tax for a period of years.

Tax Expenditure Provisions

In addition to addressing the structural problems outlined here, a thorough review of the income tax would have to confront the variety of special provisions that have been added to the law over the years to provide incentive for particular kinds of activities or to provide relief to particular kinds of taxpayers. There are about 100 such tax-expenditure provisions, more than one-quarter of which have been enacted since 1976. They include exclusions for certain kinds of income, deductions for costs other than the costs of earning income, tax credits, and tax deferral provisions.

In this regard, there are several important considerations. Tax expenditures have the advantage that they can be plugged into an administrative mechanism through which the government already communicates with a large number of its citizens. Tax expenditures do not generally require separate or detailed application forms, and they are received relatively quickly. On the other hand, most tax expenditures make the tax system more complex for the taxpayer and also reduce the extent to which the public perceives the system to be equitable. In addition, if the tax expenditure takes the form of an exclusion or deduction in a system with progressive rates, it provides a higher rate of subsidy to high-income than to low-income taxpayers, a result that may be undesirable. Unless the tax expenditure is refundable, it will not be available to taxpayers without any tax liability, and if such taxpayers are corporations, they may have a purely tax-motivated incentive to merge with taxpaying units. Tax expenditures may also cause administrative problems for the agency administering the tax system, which may be required to deal with policy issues outside its normal area of expertise. Tax expenditures have also been criticized for being, in effect, entitlement programs that are not reviewed each year as part of the appropriations process and not subject to the controls that the budget process imposes on new entitlement authority. (However, in recent years Congress has tended to put termination dates on many new tax-expenditure provisions to encourage periodic review of them.) It has been argued that, as a practical matter, some tax expenditures would not have been adopted or would have been adopted in a much more limited form if provided as budget outlays.

Analysis of tax expenditures generally involves two issues. First, whether the nontax policy goal accomplished by the tax expenditure is worth the lost revenue and whatever other tax-policy goals are being sacrificed must be decided. This is likely to be based on efficiency (benefit-cost), distributional, and administrative considerations. The second decision is whether other approaches to achieve the nontax policy goal, such as spending or regulation, would be preferable. After reviewing tax-expenditure provisions as part of an overhaul of the income tax, Congress could decide that the nontax policy goals of certain tax expenditures should be accomplished with spending programs, in which case not all the revenue raised by broadening the tax base would be available to finance tax-rate reductions. For example, if the charitable deduction were repealed, Congress might want to enact a spending program under which the federal government matches private contributions to charitable organizations. Conceivably, this matching grant program would cost as much as the revenue loss from the deduction.

ISSUES IN TRANSITION TO A NEW SYSTEM

Hypothetically, if a comprehensive income tax were enacted and made effective overnight, taxpayers would experience sharp swings in after-tax income, wealth, and cashflow. Contracts and investments that were profitable under the old tax rules could be rendered unprofitable. Taxpayers who made tax-preferred investments under the old rules could experience an abrupt decline in current (after-tax) income and in wealth—the capitalized value of future income—relative to taxpayers holding ordinary investments. This reduction in taxpayer wealth might be regarded as particularly inequitable when the shelter was designed and encouraged by Congress in order to achieve certain social or economic objectives, as in the case of tax-free municipal bonds. On the other hand, windfall losses that result from the elimination of unintended tax-avoidance practices would not necessarily be viewed as undesirable tax policy.

Sudden changes in taxpayers' after-tax incomes may also create a perception of inequity because taxpayers may find it difficult to adjust their spending patterns to the new conditions.

General Transition Rule Options

The goals of wealth protection and time-to-adjust can be achieved by two general types of transition rules: (1) grandfather clauses and (2) phase-in provisions. Grandfather clauses permit (or require) contracts and investments, initiated under the old tax rules, to be governed by the old law. If the grandfather clause is available on an elective basis, the taxpayer can avoid being made worse off as a result of the tax change; while if the clause requires old-law tax treatment, then some windfall gains resulting from the tax law change are also eliminated. A grandfathering provision may apply to all eligible investments or be limited to owners of the investment at the time the change in tax rules was first considered or enacted. If the clause is limited to the original owner, then taxpayers may not be protected against windfall losses if the investment is sold to another, ineligible investor. If the investment, rather than the owner, is grandfathered, then the owner is protected against a windfall loss even if the investment is sold after the tax-law change; indeed, since the grandfather clause creates a limited supply of old-law investments, original owners may reap windfall gains under such a rule. Also, if a tax change has been widely anticipated for a long time prior to enactment, asset values may reflect the likelihood of the change, and a grandfather rule may lead to windfall increases in asset values.

Phase-in provisions may be used to delay the effect of new tax rules on both existing and new investments. With respect to existing investments, a phase-in rule provides temporary and partial protection of asset values compared to an elective grandfather clause. The longer and more gradual a phase-in rule, the more similar it is to a grandafther clause. In the limit, if the new tax rules are only phased in after existing investments are scrapped, then the phase-in provision is precisely equivalent to a grandfather clause for existing investments. However, since many investments, such as homes, last thirty years or more, very long phase-in rules would be required to grandfather effectively all existing investments. With respect to new assets, the effect of a phase-in period is primarily to slow the rate of transition, thereby allowing taxpayers adequate time to adjust. Phase-in provisions may gradually change tax laws or simply provide a grace period in advance of a major change in rules. Both a gradual phase-in and a grace period moderate wealth changes on existing assets and provide taxpayers time to adjust.

Criteria for selecting between the alternative grandfathering and phase-in approaches include the following: (1) effectiveness in achieving the twin goals of moderating adverse wealth effects and providing taxpayers adequate time to adjust, (2) absence of incentives for taxpayers to make noneconomic, tax-motiviated investments during the transition period, and (3) simplicity of transition rules. It is unlikely that any one transition rule best satisfies all three criteria, so the choice among alternatives requires judgment about the relative importance of these objectives.

Specific Issues in the Transition to a Comprehensive Income Tax

This section surveys some of the specific transition problems associated with eliminating some of the major exclusions and deductions.

Exclusions

Some of the most important exclusions in the individual income tax are the exclusions for (1) transfer payments like Social Security and public assistance, (2) fringe benefits, and (3) 60 percent of capital gains. Including transfer payments in taxable income would reduce the benefit from these payments to those recipients whose income exceeds the level at which people begin to pay tax. It would be possible to readjust benefit schedules to compensate for inclusion in taxable income for taxpayers with a particular marginal tax rate, but this could take federal and state governments a period of several years. To allow time for such compensating legislation, it may be appropriate to delay the effective date of repeal of the exclusion for transfer payments or to phase it in. To the extent benefits are not readjusted for inclusion or the taxpayer's marginal tax rate is higher than the rate on which the benefit readjustment was based, current and future recipients would be adversely affected. This could create a problem, such as for people who have already retired or expect soon to retire on the basis of a certain level of tax-exempt retirement benefits (like Social Security). One possible response to this problem would be to grandfather retirement benefits that accrued prior to the change in the law. A drawback to grandfathering-accrued retirement benefits is the difficulty of distinguishing retirement benefits accrued before the rules changed from those accruing afterward. For this reason, it might be simpler to tax a gradually rising percentage of retirement benefits. This phase-in approach would tax least the benefits of those taxpayers nearest to retirement.

Including fringe benefits in taxable income would reduce the effective salary of employees now benefiting from fringes. Taxpayers presumably would respond by substituting cash wages for some of the less desirable fringes, but this could take time (such as to renegotiate contracts). Moreover, there will be many cases in which workers have accrued fringe benefits where realization has not taken place. The simplest transition rule would be to allow a grace period of one or more years in which realization of accrued fringe benefits could take place under the old tax law and taxpayers would have time to modify compensation arrangements.

Including 100 percent of capital gains in taxable income (without reducing tax rates) would reduce the value of many assets. The reduction in value would be largest for assets whose return is disproportionately in the form of capital gains (such as gold and homes). While accrued but unrealized capital gains could be grandfathered by applying the new rules only to appreciation occurring after the effective date (a fresh start), this would require the segregation of assets acquired prior to the law change and measurement of the market value of these assets. This approach was used when the original income tax was enacted in 1913 and when carryover of basis was enacted in 1976, but it created difficulties each time. An alternative approach would be to provide a grace period during which accrued capital gains could be realized under the present tax law. This, however, would give taxpayers an incentive to sell assets during the grace period, thereby distorting decisions. A third approach would be to retain existing law for assets owned on the effective date, but this could discourage sales of those assets. If tax rates are substantially lowered at the same time the capital-gains exclusion is eliminated, the effective rate of tax on capital gains may not increase as a result of comprehensive income tax reform, which may reduce the need for transition rules; however, there still could be declines in the values of assets whose return consists disproportionately of capital gains.

Itemized Deductions

The most important itemized deductions in the individual income tax are the deductions for interest, state and local taxes paid, charitable contributions, and medical expenses.

Eliminating the deduction for mortage interest would significantly increase the tax liability of most homeowners as well as reduce the market value of most homes. Grandfathering interest paid on existing home mortages would protect recent homebuyers from an increase in tax liability but would not prevent the present owners of the housing stock from suffering a loss in property value. To protect homeowners fully, old-law treatment would have to be accorded to the existing stock of housing in perpetuity. The transition problems associated with housing are especially difficult because housing is extremely durable and represents a large portion of taxpayer wealth. One possible transition rule would be to allow existing homeowners to take a deduction or credit for the estimated reduction in property value that resulted from the tax law change. While this would compensate the losers from eliminating the mortage-interest deduction, it would be difficult to estimate accurately the monetary loss. Alternatively, a phase in could moderate the likely decline in home prices.

Elimination of the deduction against federal income tax for certain kinds of state and local taxes paid would increase the tax liabilities of itemizing taxpayers who pay high state and local taxes. This would put some pressure on state and local governments to change their mix of tax revenues. Therefore, a grace period could be considered to give state legislatures time to make the appropriate adjustments.

Elimination of the charitable-contribution deduction could reduce the level of charitable giving, perhaps substantially. This would reduce the revenue of organizations that rely on charitable contributions and could force a reduction in their programs and outlays. A phase-in period would provide time for charitable organizations to develop alternative sources of revenues and to bring expenditure plans in line with income.

Elimination of the medical-expense deduction would increase the tax liability of itemizing taxpayers whose unreimbursed medical expenses exceed 5 percent of adjusted gross income. A phase-in or grace period could be helpful to allow taxpayers time to raise their medical insurance coverage.

The number of transition problems that arise in the adoption of a new system are numerous and often are different for the different provisions being changed. These transition problems should be considered one by one as discussions of comprehensive tax-reform progress.

NOTES

1. Jerry A. Hausman, "Labor Supply," in Henry J. Aaron and Joseph A. Pechman, eds., *How Taxes Affect Economic Behavior*, Brookings Institution, 1981.

2. It should be noted that a tax proposal that raised after-tax income could have offsetting "income" effects because some individuals would respond to their additional income by taking more leisure time. Thus the evidence of a significant substitution effect does not mean that a tax cut would necessarily increase labor supply, only that a cut in marginal tax rates offset by other changes in after-tax income would do so.

3. In 1981 there was about $57 billion of overwithholding and $35 billion of underwithholding. A change that eliminated most of the overwithholding, especially if it did not reduce the underwithholding significantly, could have major effects on budget receipts in the year it first took effect unless it were phased in.

4. For example, consider $100 of corporate-source income before taxes. There will generally be a corporate income tax of $46. If the remaining $54 is distributed as a dividend to a taxpayer in the 50-percent bracket, the individual income tax will be $27, for a combined tax burden of $73.

5. For example, consider the situations in which two corporations own stock in each other. Neither would know how much income to report until it had heard from the other how much were the other's retained earnings. Also, there would be problems in tracing audit adjustments at the corporate level through to each of the shareholders.

6. Under many integration proposals, the amount of the gross-up would be determined by a simple arithmetic formula whereby the shareholder would multiply his dividend by 1.85 regardless of the amount of tax the corporation actually paid. This is derived as follows: Assume $100 of corporate pretax income. The corporate income tax is $46, leaving $54 to be distributed as a dividend. Thus, if the shareholder multiplies his dividend by 1.85, he or she will include the full $100 in income ($\$54 \times 1.85 = 100$). The shareholder's credit, then, would be 85 percent of the dividend, or $46. If the corporation actually paid $40 owing to tax preferences, it would have to pay an additional tax of $6.

7. In 1935 Congress required the individual shareholder of each personal holding company (a U.S. corporation earning primarily passive income) to include in income his or her share of the company's undistributed earnings. In 1937 Congress enacted similar rules for foreign personal holding companies. In 1962 Congress required any 10-percent U.S. shareholder of a controlled foreign corporation to include in income

(subject to a foreign tax credit) a pro rata portion of the undistributed earnings of the foreign corporation that arise from designated activities (such as passive investment, certain related-party transactions, and certain oil-related activities).

8. The statutory fringe benefits excluded from gross income are group-term life insurance (sec. 79), a $5,000 death benefit exclusion (sec. 101(b)), accident and health plan contributions (sec. 106), the rental value of parsonages (sec. 107), meals and lodging furnished for the convenience of the employer (sec. 119), prepaid legal services (sec. 120), van pooling services (sec. 124), dependent-care assistance (sec. 129), certain in-kind benefits and cash payments to military personnel, miscellaneous benefits (sec. 132), qualified pension plans (sec. 401), and incentive stock options (sec. 422A). However, the employer is denied a deduction for the bargain element of incentive stock options.

9. Allocation would not be necessary in a flat-rate system with the corporate tax rate equal to the individual rate because businesses could simply be denied a deduction for certain fringe benefits, which could be excluded at the individual level.

10. This is not the way homeowner preferences are treated in the annual tax-expenditure budgets published by OMB, CBO, and the Joint Committee staff. In those documents, the tax expenditure for homeownership is defined as the mortgage interest and property tax deductions, on the asumption that taxing imputed rent is not a serious possibility. Only for a house that is entirely debt-financed and whose value is equal to its purchase price will the two measures of the preference be similar.

11. However, it should be noted that the United Kingdom taxed imputed rent on homes for over a century—from the beginning of its income tax to 1963. By that date, the property-value assessments on which the determination of imputed rent was based had been rendered obsolete by inflation, and the U.K. decided to exempt imputed rent rather than update the assessments.

12. Some also believe that there would be a constitutional problem with taxing unrealized gains. Canada recently adopted an elective system for taxing corporate stocks that involves taxing gains as they accrue.

13. Furthermore, the present rule under which an heir steps up the basis of inherited assets to the fair market value for estate tax purposes means that holding onto appreciated property can ultimately result in escaping any income tax on the appreciation.

14. Currently, individuals may deduct capital losses against capital gains and up to $3,000 of ordinary income. Unused capital losses may be carried forward. Corporations may not deduct capital losses against ordinary income. Their carryforward is limited to five years, but they get a three-year carryback.

15. In the Tax Equity and Fiscal Responsibility Act of 1982, the inclusion formula was revised and periodic inclusion was extended to noncorporate bonds and stripped coupon bonds. The Tax Reform Act of 1984 further extended periodic inclusion to certain debt obligations previously exempted from the 1982 provisions.

3 Uniform Tax Structures

John E. Chapoton

Uniformity in tax treatment would require consistent measurement of a clearly defined tax base. As we learned long ago, it is not enough to declare "income," or "consumed income," or "payrolls" to be the base for a tax. Accounting rules must be specified, records must be kept, and reports will be required. The kinds of rules and records needed for measuring income will be somewhat different than those required for measuring consumed income, even though there are many common elements. The differences are important enough to justify describing separately the requirements for a uniform tax on total income and those for a uniform tax on consumed income.

THE UNIFORM INCOME TAX

The Concept of Income

A precise definition of "income" is more complicated than everyday usage suggests. The correct definition when discussing taxes is "the total amount that contributes to a family's consumption in a year or adds to its net worth." Dividends and wages are clearly income,

---

This chapter is based on the author's "Statement Before The Senate Finance Committee," Flat Rate Tax Hearings Before the Committee on Finance, U.S. Senate, 97th Congress, 2d sess., 28–29 September 1982, pp. 182–97.

for example, because these receipts can be spent for consumption or used to acquire assets. Increases in vested pension rights or increases in the value of a portfolio are less obvious cases. But these are also income if they add to real net worth. By contrast, borrowing is a receipt of cash that is not income. If the proceeds are used to buy assets, there is no increase in net worth; if they are consumed, net worth is reduced by the amount borrowed.

Gray areas in applying the definition of income are a constant source of dispute in tax legislation and administration. For example, a business lunch is partly a business expense and partly an ordinary consumption expenditure. In a uniform income tax, the consumption part should be included in the income of the employee (or the self-employed), not excluded from income. The remaining portion should not be taxed. Determining the right proportions in various situations is extremely difficult.

A truly uniform income tax would require accounting for every last dollar of income, net of necessary costs. The full measurement of income would include at least the following items:

- Wage and salary receipts, net of necessary employee expenses
- Employer contributions to pension, profit-sharing, and retirement plans
- Employer contributions for health, life, or other insurance
- Earnings on all reserve funds (such as pension reserves) held for future payment of employees' benefits
- Receipts of proprietorships, net of business expenses
- A partner's allocable share of partnership income
- Rent and royalty income, net of expenses
- All dividend and interest receipts
- Transfer payments, including:
  - Social Security and railroad retirement benefits

Unemployment compensation payments
Veterans' benefits
Worker's Compensation and other disability income
Aid to Families with Dependent Children, Supplemental Security Income, and other general relief payments

- Total capital gains, net of capital losses, adjusted for inflation
- Retained corporate earnings allocated to shareholders
- Annual rental value of owner-occupied homes, net of housing-related costs

Taxation of all income does not imply the complete elimination of deductions. Any necessary costs of earning income must be deductible. This includes deduction of interest as a cost associated with debt-financed assets. Deductions for extraordinary medical costs, casualty losses, state/local taxes, and charitable contributions all may be defended on grounds that they do not represent personal consumption expenditures. The basic principle of uniform income taxation is that deductions should not be allowed to discriminate by source of income or according to consumption choices.

Uniform income is a useful standard for measuring the distribution of tax burdens and for evaluating an income tax system. Full measurement of income, however, presents a number of formidable practical problems that must be considered if a tax on uniform income is to be considered as a model for tax reform.

1. *Income accruals.* A major problem of full income measurement is that "additions to net worth" often do not coincide with cash receipts. In legal jargon, they are not "realized." When shares appreciate or pension rights increase, income has accrued, but full current measurement would require annual estimates of their values without a market transaction to confirm them. The practical alternative that has generally been followed is

to wait for a "recognition event"—a sale, exchange, or distribution—before counting the income, but this provides the familiar opportunity for tax deferral. A postponement of tax is in effect an income tax preference.

2. *Inflation adjustment.* In a period of inflation, apparent appreciation of assets may provide no income at all. This is true where the appreciation in value is just enough to maintain a family's real wealth. Any smaller appreciation is really a loss. Thus, if the $100 used to purchase a share of stock ten years ago is equivalent to $200 at today's process, no real income has been obtained unless sale of the stock brings more than $200. Accurate income measurement requires inflation adjustment for any return, or cost, that accrues over more than a year. This would mean indexing the basis for all capital assets and the face amounts of all long-term debt, which would be a formidable task.

3. *Depreciation.* An element of income measurement that has been most troublesome over the years is depreciation accounting. It is required because the loss in real value of assets is a necessary business expense—a loss of net worth. Conceptually, each physical asset should be valued in each year, and an inflation adjustment should be provided for basis. The traditional practice has been to use the familiar formulas with an estimated useful life for each broad class of assets. Inflation adjustment, while widely recognized as necessary, is not universally or consistently practiced even for purposes of business decision making. Nevertheless, accurate estimates of depreciation, adjusted for inflation, would be necessary for a uniform income tax.

4. *Integration.* One implication of the income definition is that business income ultimately belongs to families (and single individuals), not to the business entities. Increases in corporate net worth, for example, belong to the shareholders and are part of their incomes. Similarly, distributed earnings are income only to the shareholder, not also to the corporation. A uniform income tax would tax all corporate earnings according

to the circumstances of each corporate shareholder, but it would tax them only once. Thus a uniform income tax would require the integration of the corporation and individual taxes.

5. *Other practical considerations in taxing income.* Many features of the present income tax, including some that are derided as loopholes, are reactions to the inherent difficulties of income measurement. The partial exclusion of capital gains, the accelerated cost-recovery system (ACRS), and last-in, first-out (LIFO) inventory accounting are at least in part responses to the otherwise intolerable overstatement of income during periods of inflation.

Under any practical income tax, some kinds of income that are difficult to measure would have to be excluded or approximated. These include the value of employer contributions to group insurance; the value of certain services, such as checking accounts, that would be taxable if paid out in cash; and, especially, the net rental value of owner-occupied homes. Indeed, most taxpayers will refuse to believe that they derive income from their own homes. The national income accounts recognize this source of income by estimating (or imputing) the amount that homeowners earn, and automatically spend, by renting to themselves. No serious proposals for taxing income have included this item directly, although some countries have tried to do so. Some serious base-broadening proposals would disallow the deduction for mortgage interest, however, as a way of including a portion of the gross return from owner-occupied housing.

Some family expenses that do not reduce income are nonetheless widely recognized as equitable adjustments to an income tax base. Few would argue, for example, about the deduction of catastrophic medical expenses. It is also widely recognized that some allowance should be made for family size and that some minimal level of tax-free income should be allowed alike to every family of a given size.

A practical uniform income tax with no real compromises, but with minimal recognition of measurement problems, would necessarily involve considerable complexity, along with some approximations and some exclusions. It would also retain some of the present personal deductions—at least those for certain interest expenses, employee business expenses, investment expenses, and extraordinary medical costs. Thus some lack of uniformity is inevitable.

Some recent proposals, such as the one by Senator Bill Bradley and Representative Richard A. Gephardt, attempt to move toward a more uniform income tax base. But no proposals have really attempted to solve the fundamental problems of defining real investment income during inflation. Indeed, the Bradley-Gephardt proposal would make the tax less uniform in a major way by taxing fully the nominal increase in the value of capital assets, even though for any taxpayer the gains from an asset may be largely, or entirely, the result of inflation. In addition, some of the real gains are increases in corporate share values that reflect income already taxed to corporations. The Bradley-Gephardt proposal also has not addressed the other difficult problems of measuring business income or integrating the corporate tax. Another area of controversy is personal deductions. The Bradley-Gephardt proposal would continue to allow certain of these deductions, but they would not allow them uniformly for all taxpayers. For taxpayers above $40,000 of taxable income on a joint return, a portion of the deduction is effectively denied. If these deductions are necessary to assure that those of equal means are treated equally, one must ask why they should not be fully allowed at every income level.

Equity Issues

A uniform income tax would be consistent with most people's conception of equity. Those with equal incomes, regardless of the sources or uses, would pay approximately the same tax. No one could escape tax by choosing particular employers or occupations or by making particular investments.

After base broadening has been achieved and tax rates have been lowered in all classes, it would also be possible to adjust the tax-rate schedules to make them more or less progressive. However, the degree of progressivity is not a consequence of the base broadening. Instead, it should be viewed as an independent decision to change the existing distribution of tax burdens. Unlike present law, however, whatever rate structure is chosen under a uniform tax would accurately portray the distribution of tax.

Efficiency Considerations

Uniform taxation of income would remove many tax distortions from the marketplace that take place under current law. For example:

The exclusion of many fringe benefits from taxable compensation encourages workers to choose more fringe benefits than they would if all forms of compensation were taxed equally. The tax exclusion for employer-paid medical insurance is a major contributor to the over-consumption of health services and to the continuing rapid rise in health-care costs.

Preferential tax treatment among industries distorts investment decisions. For example, the capital-gains treatment for livestock or the expensing of mining costs allow those industries to attract investors in projects that yield lower pretax returns than those in other, higher-taxed industries.

The separate corporate income tax distorts economic decisions. By imposing a double tax on dividends, the corporate income tax encourages firms to issue debt rather than equity and to retain earnings rather than to pay out dividends. It also favors the unincorporated business over the corporation, and it favors industries that typically are characterized by noncorporate enterprises (principally agriculture, housing, and service industries) relative to industries dominated by corporations.

Accelerated cost recovery and the investment tax credit have reduced the excessive tax burden on investment in equipment and machines, but the income tax continues to fall heavily on investments in structures and inventories. This differential distorts choices of production methods and raises the relative tax burden on activities and industries that naturally require more of the heavily taxed capital.

Uniformity would reduce the expense and effort involved in tax planning and allow markets to choose the most productive uses of available capital. It would encourage employers to pay compensation in a form that is valuable to their workers—cold cash to consume or save as they wish. All of these represent gains in economic efficiency.

A great disadvantage of the income tax is its built-in bias against saving. The income tax discourages saving by reducing the rate of return to the saver below the market return derived from investing in capital. A taxpayer who would be willing to postpone consumption to obtain a 10 percent return, thereby making resources available for capital formation, may not be willing to make the same sacrifice for a 6 percent return, after-tax. This is not a double tax on savings, as some have asserted; it is a single tax on capital income. But this single tax has the inevitable consequence of reducing the reward for deferring consumption, and thus by making less saving available for investment, it impairs future economic growth and productivity.

Simplicity

A uniform income tax would be simpler in some respects than the present tax, but it cannot be really simple. For example, businesses with capital expenditures must account for depreciation. More accurate depreciation rules are likely to be more complicated and contentious. This is especially true in a period of inflation, which also complicates the valuing of inventories and the proper calculation of capital gains and losses. Another illustration is fringe benefits of employees. These are often close substitutes for cash wages. When they are excluded from the tax base, they provide a convenient means for avoiding tax and thus contribute to the perception of unfairness. But many fringe benefits, like the personal use of company cars, are difficult to distinguish from properly excludable business expenses, and many others, like employer-paid group insurance, are not easily valued for each employee.

Deductions and adjustments to the income of employees also complicate the measurement of the tax base, but many of these are necessary to reflect differences in ability to pay. Moving costs, employee business expenses, interest expenses, and extraordinary medical expenses may be examples. A tax system that allows too few adjustments of this type can be just as unfair (although perhaps simpler) as one with too many exclusions. Neither a uniform tax on all income nor a uniform tax on consumed income would end the complexity of measuring income. But more uniform treatment would simplify tax practice by reducing the number and importance of the fine distinctions needed to identify tax-favored activities.

The computation of tax liability can be complex under present law by income averaging, the alternative minimum tax and options of filing status, and by various tax credits, some of which have complicated limitations. A more uniform definition of the tax base and a flatter rate schedule would reduce many of these complexities.

In general, a more uniform income tax presents difficult policy trade-offs in the area of simplification. The more we attempt to make the income tax uniform in every particular, the more complicated the rules will become. The more rough and ready the rules, the more opportunities are created for otherwise unproductive tax avoidance and the more inequities are created.

Transition Considerations

Immediate implementation of a uniform tax structure would cause significant changes in the value of individuals' assets and after-tax incomes. Such changes would create windfall gains for some individuals and unfair losses for others. These changes in wealth and after-tax income can be moderated by transition rules, such as phasing-in provisions of a new law, grandfathering, and delaying effective dates. Transition rules for a uniform income tax should ensure that income is not subject to tax twice—once under the old system and a second time under the new tax law. Conversely, no tax change should leave some forms of income untaxed. For instance, the exclusion of Social Security benefits and the 60 percent exclusion of long-term capital gains could still apply to accrued but unrealized income prior to the effective date of the new law. Benefits or real gains accrued after the effective date, however, should be fully subject to tax.

Transition rules can also reduce the income and wealth redistribution resulting from changes in relative tax rates. The value of assets that currently receive favorable tax treatment, such as state and local government bonds, would fall as demand for those assets declined under a uniform tax structure. Individuals who had made specific investments because of favorable tax treatment would suffer losses. Grandfathering existing tax treatment for the life of the asset or as long as the owner retained control, or delaying the effective date, would reduce the present value of the loss on tax-favored assets.

The design of transition rules should weigh the advantages of increased efficiency and simplicity of a uniform tax structure against the wealth and income effects caused by the change in tax laws. Transition rules can reduce the amount of windfall gains and losses, but only by delaying implementation and increasing the complexity associated with the new tax system. Grandfathering assets purchased under the old law could involve delays in implementation of the new law for up to thirty years on long-lived assets. Alternatively, delaying the effective date of the new law could shorten the transition period while reducing the present value of the windfall gain or loss. During the transition period, the income tax base would be lower than the ultimate base, which would necessitate higher temporary tax rates for a given level of revenue.

UNIFORM TAX ON CONSUMED INCOME

Concept of Consumed Income

An alternative model for tax reform is a uniform tax on the amount of income consumed, rather than on the amount of income earned. The uniform tax on consumed income would differ from the uniform income tax by excluding net saving from the tax base.

This alternative model for tax reform does not represent such a radical departure from current law. In many ways, the current rules applying to saving are much closer to those required under a tax on consumed income than to rules necessary under a uniform income tax. In particular, two important sources of saving for many families—homeownership and retirement saving—are taxed almost the same way under current law as they would be taxed under a consumed income tax with a deduction for saving. Similarly, the adoption of the Accelerated Cost Recovery System in the Economic Recovery Tax Act of 1981 moved the tax treatment of business investments in machinery and equipment much closer to the treatment required under a consumed income tax. Provisions in the tax law that allow expensing of certain capital investments, such as mining exploration and development expenses, and rules that permit most costs of research and development to be expensed rather than capitalized are also consistent with a consumed income base.

The issue of whether income consumed or income earned is the appropriate base for a tax system has been debated for many years by tax theorists and social philosophers. Some prominent economists, including Professor Irving Fisher of Yale University and Professor Nicholas Kaldor of Cambridge University, have advocated some form of tax on personal consumption as a substitute for the personal income tax. The idea of taxing personal consumption rather than income has gained increasing favor and was given favorable consideration in the Treasury Department study, *Blueprints for Basic Tax Reform*, released in January 1977, and in the Report of the Meade Commission in the United Kingdom in 1978.

Under the consumed income tax, the taxpayer would include in his or her tax base all forms of current monetary income, the current consumption value of all fringe benefits supplied by employers, and the proceeds of all borrowing in excess of loan repayments. The taxpayer would be allowed to deduct from the tax base all purchases in excess of sales of income-earning assets and all deposits in excess of withdrawals in interest-bearing accounts. Accrued interest, earnings from ownership of corporate shares, increases in the value of pension and life insurance reserves, and other increases in the value of asset holdings would not be subject to tax until paid out or withdrawn for consumption.

As a simple example, a family with an income of $20,000, of which $4,000 is saved, would be taxed on $16,000, not on $20,000, as under a uniform income tax. On the other hand, if the family spent more than it earned—say $25,000—by borrowing or dipping into its savings account for the extra $5,000, it would be taxed on the $25,000 of consumption. Since total consumption in the economy is less than income, tax rates would need to be higher to generate the same amount of revenue.

The tax on consumed income would be similar in many ways to the uniform income tax and would involve many of the same base-broadening steps as compared with current law. Each taxpayer would continue to file an annual tax return that would be similar to the current Form 1040, although somewhat simpler. All forms of employee compensation (except for employer contributions to pension plans) and all personal deductions (except for interest deductions) would be treated the same as under the uniform income tax. Wages and salaries (net of necessary employee expenses), the value of employer-provided fringe benefits, and transfer payments would be included in the tax base. Personal deductions other than interest deductions and deductions necessary to measure ability to pay, such as a deduction for catastrophic medical expenses, would be eliminated. There would be no tax credits, except for the foreign tax credit. The $100 dividend exclusion, the provisions exempting from tax certain forms of interest income, such as income from All Savers certificates, and the exclusion from tax of 60 percent of recognized capital gains would all be eliminated under both the uniform income tax and the uniform tax on consumed income.

Because only individuals consume, there would be no separate corporate tax or any need to integrate personal and corporate earnings. Taxable income of an individual would include distributions from corporations and individuals' sales of corporate shares. In effect, corporate income would be taxed when it found its way into individual consumption. Retained earnings would receive no tax advantage over dividends, so attributing retentions to stockholders would be unnecessary. A tax on consumed income would, however, encourage corporations, particularly closely held corporations, to buy consumption for their employees, permitting the workers to evade taxes unless fringe-benefit rules were tightly drawn and applied.

The major differences between the two tax systems are in the treatment of saving and borrowing. Under the tax on consumed income, deductions would be allowed for all purchases of corporate shares, corporate and government bonds, shares of mutual funds and other financial instruments, assets used in a trade or business, and deposits in interest-bearing accounts. Any cash receipts from such assets, either in the form of distributed earnings, return on investment, or realized gains, would be subject to tax. Similarly, the proceeds of all borrowing would be included in the tax base, while both interest payments and repayment of loan principal would be deductible.

The inclusion of net loan proceeds in the tax base is particularly important. Otherwise, taxpayers could reduce their tax by taking a deduction for the portion of assets acquired from borrowed funds, even though the combination of borrowing and the purchase of assets does not add to net saving. The purchase price of consumer assets, such as owner-occupied homes, automobiles, and furniture, would not be deductible in the same way as business investments. While business assets yield income in the form of interest, dividends, or capital gains, consumer assets produce income in the form of services, such as the use of the house or car. For investment in business and consumer assets to be treated the same would require an estimate of the annual value of the services that the house or the car or the furniture provides—an estimate of their rental value. Since this would be extremely difficult to accomplish and difficult for the taxpayer to understand, a method that is approximately equivalent in present-value terms would be used instead. Under this method, individuals would neither include loan proceeds for these purchases in income nor be able to deduct loan repayments. In addition, the tax liability for withdrawals from savings accounts used to finance purchases of housing and automobiles might be spread out over a number of years. These special provisions would allow the tax liability arising from consumption of the services of houses, automobiles, and other major consumer durables to be spread more evenly over the useful life of the asset, rather than being assessed all at once at the time of acquisition.

The tax on consumed income would require some different, but not more complicated, reporting and record-keeping information than the uniform income tax. Taxpayers would need to report both purchases and sales of all capital assets, but there would be no need to maintain records for assets purchased in previous years because the entire sales proceeds, not just the gain, would be subject to tax upon sale. Form 1099, sent by banks and other depository institutions to report taxable interest to individuals, would be altered slightly. Instead of reporting annual interest from accounts, Form 1099 would report net withdrawals. Net withdrawals would be computed by adding together the beginning-of-year balance and interest received and then subtracting the end-of-year balance. For example, if additions to savings accounts exceeded interest earnings withdrawn from the accounts, the individual would be able to claim a deduction. There would also need to be an accounting for all loans received, but there would be no need to divide loan repayments between principal and interest, since all loan repayments would be deductible.

Equity

A uniform tax on consumed income would have some of the same equity benefits compared to current law as would a uniform tax on all income. Two individuals with the same consumed income would pay the same tax, regardless of the source of funds used for consumption or the types of consumer goods purchased.

In contrast, current law allows tax advantages for individuals who receive income in certain forms, such as transfer payments and tax-exempt fringe benefits, or who spend income on certain goods and services, such as home-insulation expenditures that qualify for residential energy credits. However, under the uniform tax on consumed income, two individuals with the same total income might pay very different amounts of tax, depending on how much each individual saved. To take an extreme example, consider a frugal person earning $100,000 a year who saves $90,000 and consumes only $10,000. Under a consumed income tax, such a person would pay the same taxes as a person who earned only $10,000 but consumed all of his earnings. A uniform income tax would tax the person earning $100,000 more than the person earning only $10,000.

This example might lead many persons to conclude that a uniform income tax is fairer than a uniform tax on consumed income because the person earning more should pay more taxes. An alternative example, however, often leads to the opposite conclusion. Consider the heir of the frugal person who earns only $10,000 but consumes $90,000 a year by selling part of his inheritance each year. Under a uniform income tax, this wealthy person with a high standard of living will pay the same tax as a poorer person earning and spending $10,000 a year. The consumed income tax, however, places a heavier tax burden on the person spending $100,000 a year, even though that person earns only $10,000. Thus, compared to a uniform income tax, the consumed income tax falls less heavily on the person who lives frugally and accumulates wealth and more heavily on the person who lives well by selling wealth. The uniform income tax has the opposite effect in that it places a higher tax burden on the person who accumulates wealth than on the person who spends it.

These examples do not clearly demonstrate whether or not a consumed income tax is less equitable than a uniform tax on all income. There is, however, a further issue. In many cases, wealth is not spent by later generations but indeed is increased from generation to generation. Under the consumed income tax, such growing estates would never be subject to income taxation. If this is a matter of concern, an estate tax could be designed as a complement to the consumed income tax to limit the tax-free accumulation of wealth over many generations. Under a uniform income tax, or even under the current tax system, an estate tax imposes a double tax on wealth, because accumulations of wealth are taxed as income is saved. One's attitude toward an estate tax might be much different under a consumed income tax, since there would be no double tax on wealth. In that case, some might be more willing to use an estate tax to provide a single tax on the transfer of large estates.

Distribution of Tax Burdens

A uniform tax on consumed income would allow personal exemptions for taxpayers and could tax the remaining consumed income, in excess of exemptions, at either a single rate or with a graduated structure involving several rate brackets. A tax on consumed income is not inherently more or less favorable to high-income households than a uniform income tax, even though low-income households generally consume a larger fraction of their income than high-income households. Under either uniform tax system, the distribution of the tax burden among taxpayers with different abilities to pay could be altered by changing the basic exemption level and the rate structure.

Efficiency

A uniform tax on consumed income would also have many of the same benefits in improved economic efficiency as would a uniform tax on all income. Under either form of uniform taxation, the tax system would no longer bias choices among investment projects, methods of finance, and different consumption goods. Both tax systems would be neutral among different types of capital investments, neutral between debt and equity finance, neutral between corporate and noncorporate forms of enterprise, and neutral between consumer goods and services generally and certain goods and services, such as medical insurance, that receive tax benefits under current law.

A further advantage of a tax on consumed income is that, unlike the uniform income tax, it would not cause a disincentive for saving and capital formation. Since saving is exempted from the tax base, all consumption would be taxed when it occurs, whether financed from the proceeds of current earnings or from the proceeds of accumulated savings. In contrast, under a uniform income tax, consumption made possible by past saving is taxed *before* it occurs, when the income is earned. The present value of taxes can be lowered by moving the timing of consumption forward, either by reducing saving or by increasing borrowing.

Compared to a uniform income tax, a tax on consumed income would probably result in a higher saving rate, leading to increased capital formation, a higher growth rate in the short run, and a permanently higher level of output in the long run. However, the exclusion of savings from the tax base also means that a tax on consumed income would require slightly higher tax rates to raise the same revenue as a uniform tax on all income. Higher tax rates would increase the disincentive to work to obtain current consumption goods and would worsen the distortions from any preferences that might remain in the tax system. Treasury's estimates indicate that the rate differential would not be large, so the impact of the differential would also be small.

Simplicity

A tax on consumed income would be much simpler than a uniform income tax, even though some new reporting requirements would be added. Its main advantage is that it avoids many of the severe problems in measuring the tax base that are encountered under a uniform tax on all income. Another benefit from taxing income only when consumed rather than when earned is that there would be no need to account for changes in the value of assets between two different tax years. Thus there would be no need for complex rules for depreciation accounting, no need to adjust the measurement of capital income for inflation, and no need for complex rules to allocate corporate retained earnings among shareholders and to allocate accumulations of pension fund and life insurance reserves among policyholders. All purchases of productive assets would be immediately deductible in the year purchased. There would be no separate tax on the income of corporations—only a tax on distributions from corporations to individuals and on sales of corporate shares. Since all assets would be purchased with pretax dollars, the entire sales proceeds, not only the gain, would be subject to tax.

Other Consumption Taxes

One version of a flat tax that approximates a uniform tax on consumed income is S. 2147, introduced by Senator Dennis DeConcini of Arizona. S. 2147 is based on the flat tax proposal developed by Robert Hall and Alvin Rabushka of the Hoover Institution. Under S. 2147 there would be a single-rate tax on employee compensation and on business cash flow. Corporations and noncorporate business entities would be taxed on total revenues less purchases of assets, wages, and purchases of goods and services from other firms. Dividends and interest payments would not be deductible in computing the business tax, nor would they be includible in the income of the recipient. S. 2147 would, in effect, tax most of the consumed income of individuals, other than consumption from wages, at the enterprise level. The single tax rate makes it possible to use cash flow of business enterprises as a proxy for the cash flow of owners and creditors of business firms. Such a simplifying device could not be used in any system with graduated rates or individual exemptions that apply to consumption out of past savings as well as to current wage income.

Another way of taxing consumption is to collect the entire tax from business firms, either in the form of a retail sales tax or as a tax on value added at each stage of production. A retail sales tax or a value-added tax, if sufficiently general, could be designed to have the same total tax base as the uniform tax on consumed income. However, any tax on business sales could not adequately take account of variations in individuals' ability to pay. By its very nature, such a tax could not maintain the overall progressivity of the current income tax and could not provide basic personal exemptions for low-income households. In contrast, the uniform tax on consumed income would achieve the major benefits of a sales tax—simplicity and improved savings incentives—without necessarily redistributing the tax burden from high-income to low-income families.

Transition Rules

As in the case of the uniform income tax, movement toward a uniform tax on consumed income would involve significant changes in the distribution of wealth and income that could be limited by transition rules. Transition rules for a uniform tax on consumed income are especially important to ensure that income does not escape taxation and is not subject to tax twice. Older persons could be subject to double taxation if their consumption during retirement depends on wealth accumulated out of after-tax income. Treating all existing wealth as though it were tax-paid, however, would result in income from certain assets escaping taxation completely, since many existing assets would have been purchased with pretax dollars. This is true, for example, of individual retirement and Keogh accounts, benefits received under qualified pension or profit-sharing plans, and untaxed accumulations, such as unrealized capital gains or accrual of life insurance reserves.

Transition rules for a uniform consumed-income tax would require the same trade-offs among equity, efficiency, and simplicity as transition rules for a uniform income tax. For instance, designation of existing wealth as tax-paid assets would not require measuring existing wealth, but it would allow some consumption to escape taxation completely. Identifying and measuring assets according to whether they were established out of pretax or after-tax income would be administratively difficult. Delaying the implementation of the consumed income tax would require higher taxes on consumption during the transition period and would reduce the present value of efficiency gains from the imposed tax system.

A uniform tax based on consumed income has considerable appeal as a model for tax reform. It would allow for important simplifications in the taxation of the return to savings and would remove the disincentive to saving that exists under both current law and a uniform income tax. However, a tax on consumed income would be considered inequitable by some because it would allow wealth to be accumulated tax-free. It would also require higher tax rates to raise the same revenue than would a uniform income tax, although elimination of many deductions, exclusions, and credits would result in lower tax rates than current rates.

CONCLUSION

There are two models for evaluating flat-tax proposals: the income tax and the consumed-income tax. The current tax code is a hybrid of the two structures, but it contains a substantial number of provisions that are inconsistent with both models. In fact, it is impossible to say whether current law is closer to a uniform income tax or to a uniform tax on consumed income. Many recent changes in the tax laws and many proposed reforms have been consistent with one or both of the uniform structures.

Recent actions have been taken to expand the tax base. The move in 1978 to tax a portion of unemployment compensation is a good example. Any such change is in line with both concepts of uniformity. There have also been actions to encourage saving for special purposes, such as the expansion of the availability and uses of IRAs and Keoghs. These move the tax law closer to a consumed-income tax and further away from a uniform income tax. The important accelerated-cost-recovery provisions enacted in the Economic Recovery Tax Act of 1981 again moved the tax structure toward a tax on consumed income.

There have been other changes in the law to require better matching of income and related deductions. Such reforms are consistent only with an income tax. Recent tax-law changes dealing with completed contract accounting, capitalization of construction-period interest and taxes related to real property, and the cutback of deductions for mineral exploration costs and intangible drilling and development costs all represent shifts toward a uniform income tax. Not all recent revisions in the tax laws have been consistent with the two models, however. Provisions such as the expansion of the general interest exclusion, the exclusion of interest on All Savers certificates, credits for energy exploration, research and development, and earned income would appear in neither of the two structures.

Any future changes in the structure of our taxes should be based on a clear understanding of uniform structures. Anyone addressing fundamental tax reform needs to have a uniform framework in mind. Most proposals touted as basic tax reform are incomplete and contain features that move in exactly the wrong direction. This misdirection is not for lack of lofty objectives. Rather, it appears to result from the lack of a uniform framework that will require making very tough, unpopular decisions along with the easy ones.

4 The Fair Tax

Bill Bradley

TAX RATES

The objective of the Fair Tax is to reduce tax rates as much as possible. Every loophole repeal must be considered in light of the lower rates that the package makes possible; the pain of giving up a tax benefit can be more than offset by the lower rates that come along in the bargain. As Senator Joe Biden of Delaware said at the introduction of the Fair Tax Act of 1983: "Some of the changes proposed I could not support on an individual basis. But I can support them if they are part of a comprehensive package to restore fairness, simplicity, and economic sense to our taxing system."

So let's start with the good news. The main part of the Fair Tax Act is a simple 14 percent tax on *taxable* income. This means that you merely take your total income (what is called *adjusted gross* income in tax jargon), subtract your personal exemptions and your standard deduction (or itemized deductions, if applicable), and multiply the result by 0.14. And for about 80 percent of all taxpayers—families with total incomes under $40,000 and single persons under $25,000—that is the end of the story.

The 14 percent rate is equal to the *very lowest* tax-bracket rate before the 1981 Reagan tax cuts. While it

---

This chapter is based on Chapter 8 of the author's *The Fair Tax* (New York: Pocket Books, 1984).

is higher than the lowest 11 percent rate today, low-income taxpayers are still better off under the Fair Tax's 14 percent rate because of substantial increases in the personal exemption and the standard deduction.

So for about four out of five taxpayers, the Fair Tax is as simple as a flat tax. There is no wondering how much tax will be due on an hour of overtime, a cost-of-living raise, or earnings from a second job—it is exactly 14 percent. And there will be no marriage penalty and no bracket creep for taxpayers because there are no brackets.

But a flat tax for everyone would be a bonanza for the wealthiest taxpayers. Even under the current tax law, with all its loopholes, taxpayers with over $200,000 pay an average of about 25 percent of their income in tax. (Obviously, some pay a lot more, and others pay a lot less.) A 14 percent flat tax would be Christmas on April 15 for those taxpayers. But more to the real point, it would leave the federal government short of revenue, forcing an increase in the tax rate; that would give the average taxpayer higher taxes to finance a still larger tax cut for those who are better off.

So the Fair Tax cannot stop with the 14 percent basic tax. There is also an additional tax (or "surtax") similar to the structure of the original income tax of 1913. It equals 12 percent of *adjusted gross* income between $40,000 and $65,000 for families (between $25,000 and $37,500 for single persons), and 16 percent of *adjusted gross* income above $65,000 for couples ($37,500 for single people). The surtax is paid *in addition to* the basic tax; thus the *combined* tax rates of the Fair Tax are 14 percent (on *taxable* income under $40,000), 12 percent (on *total* income from $40,000 to $65,000, which gives a combined rate of 26 percent), and 16 percent (on *total* income above $65,000, which gives a combined rate of 30 percent). This 30 percent maximum rate, of course, is sharply lower than the top 50 percent rate under current law.

The reason why the Fair Tax has this very different pattern of a separate basic tax and surtax is that this pattern results in total tax revenue equal to that under the current tax law, *with each income group paying the same amount as it does now.* For example, persons making between $40,000 and $50,000 pay as a group the same percent of total income taxes as they do under current law. The Fair Tax is not a disguised redistribution scheme within income groups; however, there will be winners and losers, depending on how much they have used tax gimmicks to reduce their income subject to tax. And 70 percent of the taxpayers will pay less tax.

Having the two separate taxes may seem to be more complicated than the current tax law, but it is not. The surtax will not affect 80 percent of all taxpayers, and they will find out in the simplest possible way—from the amount of their total income. For that 80 percent there is only one tax rate. And the surtax is on *total* income. There are no special deductions to compute.

This last point is important in another connection. The surtax is on *total* income, so deductions don't count. This means that people with high total incomes cannot avoid their fair share of income taxes by loading up on itemized deductions. The Fair Tax doesn't work that way. It also has an effect on everyone with incomes above the surtax level who itemize deductions.

INCOME

The Fair Tax closes many loopholes through which income escapes tax under the current law. The first provision of the Fair Tax, which affects primarily middle-income taxpayers, is the exclusion for employer-paid health and life insurance premiums. The second, which affects primarily upper-income taxpayers, is the exclusion for part of long-term capital gains. The third is special tax breaks for the oil and gas industries.

When employers pay all or part of the life or health insurance premiums of their employees, the employers may deduct those costs, just like cash wages, for purposes of computing their business taxes. There is nothing wrong with that; it is part of the cost of hiring labor and so is a legitimate business expense. But unlike cash wages, the employer-paid insurance premiums are not considered taxable income of the employee. This causes two problems.

First, it isn't fair. Consider one worker who receives generous fringe benefits of this kind—fully prepaid health, dental, and life insurance—from his employer, while another worker who gets the same cash wages receives no fringe benefits. They pay the same taxes, but the first worker is clearly better off; the second has to pay out of pocket for his medical insurance, or for the medical bills themselves. Those insurance premiums are *income* for the 43 million workers in America who benefit from them, and the tax system should recognize that. The average employer-provided health insurance in America costs $1,000 per worker and ranges from $400 per person in the retail industry to $1,600 or higher per person in some primary industries.

Second, excluding those insurance premiums from tax makes them better than cash—and so workers have been maneuvering to get more of their pay in that form. In the twenty years from 1962 to 1982, fringe benefits like life and health insurance premiums have grown from 7.5 percent of total employee compensation of corporations to 17 percent. That is a classic example of the growth of a loophole reducing the amount of income subject to tax and forcing tax rates up.

I'd like to let every worker keep the exclusion for his employer-paid insurance premiums. And I'd like to cut the taxes on everybody's cash income too. But we can't do both. Congress must get tax rates down and still maintain federal government revenues. So the Fair Tax repeals the exclusion for employer-paid insurance premiums and taxes them as income under the income tax.

Clearly, we will have to do a lot of adjusting if employer-paid insurance premiums are taxable. Right now, nobody pays much attention to the insurance premiums; they are like mad money because nobody has to pay taxes on them. Employees will have to think more carefully about how much coverage they want, and employers will have to offer more options. Both will have to search more carefully for the best values in insurance plans. These will be healthy changes, and the federal government should cooperate and encourage the process. But the real payoff is that the tax rates will come down in the bargain. For many employees their total tax bill will be less under the Fair Tax, even without the insurance-premium exclusion, because the tax rates will be so low.

The second example of an income tax exclusion under current law is that for long-term capital gains. Capital gains are the profits from buying and selling assets such as stocks, bonds, commodity futures, and precious metals. If such assets are held more than six months, only 40 percent of the capital gain is taxed. (In tax jargon, there is an exclusion of 60 percent of long-term capital gains.) This means that the highest tax rate on capital gains is 20 percent (that is, 40 percent of the top ordinary tax rate of 50 percent).

Unlike employer-paid insurance premiums, which primarily benefit middle-income people, capital gains are the domain of the wealthy. In 1981, according to the most recent IRS data, taxpayers with more than $1 million of adjusted gross income received 56 percent of their total income in the form of capital gains. This far exceeds the share of capital gains in any lower-income group. This means that 56 percent of million-dollar-plus incomes is taxed at a top rate of only 20 percent. Yet a single wage-earner making a mere $24,500 a year pays a top rate of 30 percent.

Congressmen and senators on the tax-writing committees always hear clamoring for lighter taxation of capital gains: reducing the minimum holding period to less than six months or even eliminating it entirely; or increasing the exclusion to 70, 80, 90, or even 100 percent. The people pushing these ideas do have a point. Lighter taxation of capital gains does encourage investment in capital assets, which can increase productivity. And someone who holds a capital asset for a long time may find his nominal dollar gain large, but because of inflation his increase in *real* purchasing power will be small.

But there is another side to this coin. Investors in capital assets have the choice of selling their assets whenever they want. They can sell some assets that have gone up and others that have gone down at the same time, so that taken together there is no gain to be taxed. Then they can simply hold other assets that have gone up in value, letting their capital gains compound themselves with no tax due at all. They can sell in some years when they happen to be in a low tax bracket, so that the tax is smaller; or they can just hold on until death, when the asset can be passed on to an heir with no income tax due at all (only an estate tax, if necessary, is paid). So our capital-gains tax is really a rough-justice compromise with the investor; the investor loses on some parts of the compromise, but he does win on others.

Also, like all tax incentives, the capital-gains exclusion is prone to leakage. This means that the incentive can be used by people who are not serving the purpose the incentive was intended to promote. For example, investors in businesses can make the economy more productive and competitive, but speculators in precious metals and antiques, who do nothing for our competitiveness, get the very same capital-gains exclusion.

We certainly want low taxes on capital gains to encourage capital formation. In fact, in the 1981 tax bill, I offered an amendment to lower the capital-gains tax to 15 percent. But we also want low taxes on wages, interest, dividends, and every other reward to productive activity. There is no obvious reason why one form of income should be favored over the others by the tax system. So the Fair Tax eliminates the capital-gains exclusion as a part of the effort to get the marginal tax rate on all income as low as possible. This means that capital gains will be taxed at the same 14, 26, and 30 percent rates as all other income.

The Fair Tax's repeal of the capital-gains exclusion will not slow investment or capital formation. For one thing, the highest 30 percent tax rate is not much more than the 28 percent capital-gains rate that was in effect from 1979 to 1981. When the capital gains rate was cut to 28 percent, investors hailed the dawning of a new age of capital formation and growth; if 28 percent was so good, 30 percent can't be much worse. Also, while the maximum tax rate on capital gains is increasing from 20 to 30 percent, the maximum rate on interest and dividends—other important rewards for investors—is *falling* from 50 to 30 percent. The top rate on *short-term* capital gains (on assets held less than six months) also falls from 50 to 30 percent. And there is no longer any need to hold an asset for at least six months to obtain the most favorable tax treatment, so investors can trade their assets as frequently as they wish. On balance, it's a good deal for investors and investment.

Finally, the corporate income tax is at least as important as the tax on capital gains in determining the amount of business investment that takes place. I will explain later how the Fair Tax revises the corporate income tax not only to reduce tax sheltering and improve the targeting of business investment but also to increase the quantity of investment.

The third series of loopholes benefits the oil and gas industry. Like other industries of fuel and nonfuel minerals, it fares extremely well under the Internal Revenue Code. This is primarily because of two generous preferences: percentage depletion and the so-called intangible drilling cost deduction.

The depletion allowance is to oil and gas what depreciation is to equipment. The tax law properly recognizes that capital is consumed when oil and gas or other minerals are extracted from the ground. So it provides a depletion deduction to compensate for the exhaustion of these "wasting assets" consumed in producing income.

The problem is that for many taxpayers, the amount of the deduction bears little relationship to the amount of the oil and gas produced, or even to what it cost the producer to acquire the oil and gas property. Instead, the allowance is based on an arbitrary percentage formula that often permits the taxpayer to deduct more than his income from a particular oil- or gas-producing well year after year. Moreover, a taxpayer can claim percentage depletion indefinitely, even though he may have long since recovered the full amount of his investment in the oil and gas property. In sum, it is an outright subsidy to invest in oil and gas drilling. And its availability has spawned some of the most lucrative tax shelters going.

The other special tax break near and dear to the heart of the petroleum industry is the deduction for intangible drilling costs. These ephemeral-sounding expenditures are actually expenses incurred in developing oil and gas wells. Normally, the Internal Revenue Code says that if a taxpayer makes an expenditure to acquire or permanently improve income-producing property, he can't deduct that expenditure all in one fell swoop. Rather, he has to deduct a portion each year based on the useful life of the property involved. Not so with oil and gas development expenditures—they can be deducted immediately and in full. This special treatment, especially in combination with percentage depletion, results in inordinately generous treatment for the petroleum industry, while the rest of the taxpayers are left with punitively high rates.

Employer-paid insurance, capital gains, and oil and gas are three areas where the Fair Tax makes some tough choices. These tax breaks, and most of the others, seem well intentioned and harmless. Piled on top of one another, however, they narrow the tax base and force us to use higher tax rates to collect the revenue we need. The high rates choke off economic incentives, encourage tax gamesmanship, and leave various groups begging for *more* tax loopholes.

We must break out of this vicious cycle. The Fair Tax shows up front the loopholes that we must give up and the lower tax rates that will be our reward.

DEDUCTIONS

Besides the exclusions of some types of income, the current tax law allows deductions to provide relief for certain taxpayers. Here again, the Fair Tax makes some definite improvements and some tough choices.

The most basic deduction under the current law is a $1,000 exemption for every taxpayer (husband and wife are both taxpayers) and dependent (children count as dependents). The $1,000 exemption has not been changed since 1978, and inflation has greatly reduced its value since then. The Fair Tax increases the exemption for a taxpayer to $1,600; the exemption for a dependent remains at $1,000. Thus a husband-wife family of four can claim two $1,600 taxpayer exemptions and two $1,000 dependent exemptions, for a total of $5,200 (instead of $4,000 under current law). Under the Fair Tax, that family can earn $1,200 more without paying any tax. (Single-parent families get a special $1,750 taxpayer exemption to compensate for their higher costs of living.)

A second form of relief under the current tax law is the "zero-bracket amount," or standard deduction. Even if a taxpayer does not itemize his deductions, he can claim the standard deduction and exempt that much income from tax. About two-thirds (more than 60 million) of all taxpayers claim the standard deduction now. Under the current law, the standard deduction for couples is $3,400 (so a family of four with four $1,000 exemptions can earn $7,400 without paying tax). Inflation has eaten away at the standard deduction in the last few years, just as it has the exemptions.

The Fair Tax increases the $3,400 standard deduction for couples to $6,000. For single persons, the deduction increases from $2,300 to $3,000. This means that families of four can earn $11,200 ($5,200 in personal exemptions plus the $6,000 standard deduction) before paying any tax, compared to $7,400 under the current tax law.

The higher personal exemptions and standard deductions under the Fair Tax will remove from the tax rolls many people with low incomes. Without the Fair Tax many people who are officially defined as poor would be paying income taxes. Other people just a bit better off will have their taxes significantly reduced, and even people with $15,000 to 20,000 incomes will benefit from a bigger standard deduction and exemption. These people were hardly helped by the 1981 tax-rate cuts for people with higher incomes.

The big increase in the standard deduction will also simplify tax filing for many people. Two million taxpayers who now itemize deductions just greater than the current standard deduction will be able to claim the bigger standard deduction under the Fair Tax. They will get a larger deduction, and they won't have to go through the hassles of itemizing—keeping records and filling out forms.

MARRIAGE PENALTY

Another important effect of the Fair Tax is how it reduces the so-called marriage penalty—the tendency of the current tax law to increase the combined taxes of two working people who get married. One reason this happens now is because spouses, separately, can claim a $2,300 standard deduction as single taxpayers, so together their total tax-free income is $4,600; but when they marry and file jointly, they can claim only one $3,400 standard deduction. The penalty results in part from this $1,200 drop in their total standard deduction. Because the Fair Tax has a standard deduction for couples that is exactly twice that for single people ($6,000 vs. $3,000), there is no such drop. Another reason for the marriage penalty is that the couple's incomes added together push them into higher tax brackets; but the Fair Tax has many fewer brackets. Because of these structural changes, the Fair Tax has no marriage penalty whatever for couples with combined incomes under $40,000. They pay a simple 14 percent tax. Even with the "two-earner couple deduction" under the current law, a couple at the $40,000 level now has a marriage penalty of as much as $2,730. It is even higher when one considers that many eligible couples have not been claiming the two-earner deduction, perhaps because it's so complicated. (It is equal to 10 percent of the earnings of the lesser-earning spouse, with a maximum deduction of $3,000.) Above the $40,000 income level, marriage penalties under the Fair Tax are almost always lower, even though it repeals the "two-earner" deduction. (There is still some penalty because of the Fair Tax's progressive rates.) The highest marriage penalty under the Fair Tax is $1,600; the highest under the current law, even with the special deduction is $4,048. For those who take advantage of the special deduction, the penalty under current law is even higher.

The present tax law *indexes the personal exemptions and zero-bracket amounts in 1985,* to keep them even with inflation. The Fair Tax does not provide for automatic indexation for four reasons. First, the Fair Tax already increases these deductions far more than would indexation. Indexation would increase these amounts by an expected 5 percent rate of inflation in 1985, but the Fair Tax increases the taxpayer exemptions by 60 percent, and the standard deductions by 30 percent for single persons and 76 percent for couples. Second, because the Fair Tax has only three tax rate brackets (and 80 percent of all taxpayers are in only the first bracket), the problem of "bracket creep" is largely eliminated by the basic structure of the tax. Third, the Congress has always cut taxes under its own discretion to compensate for inflation, and I am sure that under the Fair Tax it will continue to do so. But we will be better off structurally because the inflation dividend can be used for further rate reduction instead of more special-interest loopholes. Finally, there might be a time when we will want to consider holding back on tax cuts in order to close the deficit or putting them into effect, in order to give the economy a boost.

Itemized Deductions

About one-third (over 30 million) of all taxpayers now itemize their deductions rather than claiming the standard deduction. To bring tax rates down, the Fair Tax cuts back on some of the itemized deductions.

The Fair Tax repeals the deduction for state and local sales taxes. It also repeals all state and local tax deductions except the income tax and property tax deductions. The income tax deduction is needed to avoid "double taxing" income; the property tax deduction is retained as part of the long-term agreement between the federal government and homeowners. The mortgage interest deduction is retained for the same reason.

The deduction for interest other than on mortgages is cut back, however. Taxpayers may claim nonmortgage interest deductions only up to the amount of their investment income. In other words, interest expense (other than mortgage interest) is deductible for purposes of both the basic tax and the surtax, but only to the extent that it offsets interest income or other investment income.

The itemized deduction for medical expenses is trimmed back. Only medical-care costs in excess of 10 percent of income are deductible, compared to the current law's 5 percent. The medical-expense deduction is cut back because inflation in health-care costs now allows for a deduction for routine as opposed to extraordinary costs. And the income tax cannot be a first line of defense against health-care costs. The medical-expense deduction does not help low-income people, because they seldom itemize their deductions anyway; such people are helped by the Fair Tax through the big increases in the exemptions and standard deductions. Most middle-income working people have employer-provided insurance and moderate other medical bills; they would be better off with lower tax rates and bigger exemptions than with a small medical-expense deduction. For those with very large medical bills, no tax deduction can cover the financial loss fully, because a tax deduction only reduces taxes by a fraction of the expense equal to the tax rate. So a deduction for $1 of medical expenses under the Fair Tax saves the taxpayer 14 cents. The deduction under the Fair Tax still provides some relief from catastrophic medical expenses, but the only real protection from medical costs is adequate insurance, not a tax deduction.

The Fair Tax keeps the most important and widely used deductions—for mortgage interest, property and income taxes, and charitable contributions. In terms of itemized deductions, the Fair Tax isn't a radical change, although some people will reduce their taxes by switching from itemized deductions to the standard deduction. There is a change, however, in the handling of itemized deductions for all taxpayers in the surtax income range—about $40,000 for married couples and $25,000 for single persons. The surtax is collected against *total* income, not *taxable* income, so the itemized deductions do not reduce the surtax. There are two reasons why the Fair Tax uses this arrangement.

First, on principle, I believe that above a certain income level people should have to pay a certain fraction of their income in tax, regardless of their itemized deductions, *if the tax rates are reasonable*. In the Fair Tax, the tax rates are very low, and so the separate surtax is a reasonable contribution from people to keep their government running. And people cannot evade the Fair Tax by piling up itemized deductions. The surtax doesn't allow them. The only exception to this restriction of deductions from the surtax is interest expense as it applies against investment income. If a taxpayer subject to the surtax is both borrowing (and therefore paying interest) and lending (and therefore receiving interest income), his or her interest deduction should apply at the same tax rate at which the interest income is taxed. Therefore, interest expense, in amounts not greater than investment income, is deductible under the surtax.

Second, under the Fair Tax, everyone's itemized deductions count against the same 14 percent basic tax, and so everyone's deductions are worth the same amount: 14 cents on the dollar. So the Fair Tax has a different philosophy toward itemized deductions. Homeownership is a good thing, and the tax system should encourage it. But the Fair Tax deductions contribute to everyone's mortgage interest and property taxes to the same degree—14 cents on the dollar. It isn't like the current law, when a top-bracket taxpayer's mortgage interest is reimbursed by the federal government at 50 cents on the dollar, but a dollar of a low-income taxpayer's mortgage is worth as little as 11 cents. No longer will the tax system give more in reduced taxes to the wealthy than to the middle class. These "upside-down subsidies" are eliminated by the Fair Tax.

In practice, all of this works out simply. There is no change at all for four out of five taxpayers whose incomes are below the surtax cutoffs of $40,000 for married couples and $25,000 for single persons. (That is, 80 percent of all taxpayers just claim deductions and compute the basic tax at 14 percent.) Taxpayers above the surtax range simply compute the additional surtax on total income, and it's done.

So on income above $40,000 (or $25,000 for single persons), what's in this for middle-income taxpayers? Why should they want the Fair Tax if their itemized deductions are worth only 14 cents on the dollar?

The anwer is the same as the goal of the Fair Tax: lower tax rates. The highest tax rate under the Fair Tax is 30 percent. The highest tax rate under the current tax law is 50 percent. That is a cut of 20 percentage points, or 40 percent. The Fair Tax rates are lower in part because there is a relation between the amount of tax deductions we allow and the tax rates we must charge. If we duck the Fair Tax's horsetrade on deductions, we will be stuck with the same high tax rates we have today.

While some people are better off under a high tax rate–high tax preference system, most of us are simply bewildered and angry with the maze of IRS regulations. Once during a radio call-in show, a constituent volunteered that he supported the Fair Tax. He told me that his next-door neighbor who earned about the same income as he did paid an effective tax rate of 6 percent while the caller paid 38 percent, and he continued that the neighbor thought he was stupid because he didn't take advantage of tax gimmicks. The caller went on to say he was a chemist and preferred to do what he did best in the laboratory rather than look for tax breaks. With the Fair Tax, he concluded, he would pay his fair share but could be assured that his neighbor would also.

Under the Fair Tax, 70 percent of our 100 million taxpayers will pay less tax, and virtually every taxpayer will have a substantial reduction in his or her marginal tax rate—the tax that must be paid on an extra dollar of income. This means that taxpayers can keep more of the extra income they earn from extra work, a promotion, or a cost-of-living raise. It will give the taxpayer a greater incentive to work more and invest more, knowing that he or she will never have to pay more than 30 percent of the next dollar of income in federal income taxes. It is good for the American taxpayer—and good for the whole economy.

HOW THE FAIR TAX WORKS

So after all of the reengineering, what is the Fair Tax? We should probably start to answer that question with what the Fair Tax is not: (a) The Fair Tax is not a traditional tax cut, even though 70 percent of all taxpayers will pay less. It will collect the same revenue as the current tax law in its first year, with no supply-side "rosy scenario" involved. And in fact, because it ends some tax exclusions that now shrink the tax base and will expand in the future, the Fair Tax will collect *more* revenue than the current law in later years. (b) The Fair Tax is not a redistribution scheme. It will collect the same revenue from each income group, as is done now.

So the Fair Tax *is* a plan to close tax loopholes and reduce tax rates—together. It does not pander to any one group; it touches just about everyone's loopholes, and it lowers everyone's tax rates. So it increases everyone's incentives to work, invest, and save, which is good for the economy. And it determines everyone's taxes at low, fair rates without loopholes for some people to duck their fair share, which is good for the country.

THE CORPORATE INCOME TAX

Most people probably know that we have a corporate income tax, but very few know much about it. About the only attention the corporate tax has gotten in recent years was the furor over the so-called safe harbor leasing—the device in the Reagan tax cuts that allowed corporations to buy and sell tax breaks. As it happens, safe harbor leasing, even though it has since been repealed, is still a good example of what is wrong with the corporate tax and how the Fair Tax works better.

In principle, the corporate income tax should operate just like the individual income tax: You measure income, and you tax it. The problem is that corporate income is usually harder to measure than a family's income. The reason is that corporate income is earned through investments that last more than one year. If a young entrepreneur opens a street-corner lemonade stand and he spends one dollar making lemonade that he sells for three dollars, his income is obviously two dollars. But if a corporation invests $1 million in a factory that earns (after other costs) $200,000 in the first year, did the corporation lose $800,000? Not if the factory can operate for nine more years before it wears out. The corporation has to be allowed to earn $1 million free of tax to recover its original investment, but not necessarily in the first year.

The proper method, in theory, is to allow tax deductions equal to the amount of the investment, spread over the *useful life* of the investment; so for the $1 million factory lasting ten years, the firm might be allowed a $100,000 *depreciation* deduction each year for ten years. This simple procedure has one big hitch, though; over those ten years, inflation can greatly reduce the value of those $100,000 deductions, so the deductions will not yield a large enough reserve to replace the factory. A $1 million factory in 1970 could not be built for $1 million in 1980. For this reason the deductions are usually allowed faster than over the expected life of the asset so that they can be reinvested sooner, to earn more interest and make up for inflation. In the example above, the factory might be depreciated over six years instead of ten. This process is called *accelerated* depreciation. The more accelerated the depreciation is, the more generous it is to the investing firm, and the sooner the firm has use of the cash freed up by depreciation.

Another device in the tax law to compensate for inflation and also to encourage firms to invest is the investment tax credit. For most investments in machinery, firms receive a tax credit equal to 10 percent of the price. In effect, the federal government pays 10 percent of the cost of the machine by reducing the corporation's taxes by the commensurate amount. The idea is that firms will invest more to get the tax break, and so the economy will be more productive.

As part of Reaganomics, the 1981 tax cut greatly accelerated business depreciation allowances and in some cases increased the investment tax credit. These changes were so extremely generous that they would clearly wipe out many corporations' tax liabilities altogether. And that raised a problem: If General Motors, for example, would save a lot of cash by making an investment and collecting the generous tax breaks, but Chrysler, for example, wouldn't save any cash because they had run years of losses and so didn't owe taxes in the first place, wouldn't that encourage GM to invest and expand and Chrysler to stagnate? And so was born safe harbor leasing—a scheme to allow the Chryslers of the economy to sell investment tax breaks they couldn't use to the GMs, who could.

In my view, there was a big problem. But it *wasn't* safe harbor leasing. It was the huge depreciation deductions and investment tax credits that put firms that were rebuilding, such as Chrysler and also many new, up-and-coming firms, at a competitive disadvantage in the first place.

And the depreciation formulas adopted in the 1981 tax cuts are terribly biased; they lump most machinery into one big class with the same assumed useful life, regardless of the actual useful life of the machine. This means that some investments in machinery are treated generously, but others are treated *extremely* generously. Depending on how long their equipment lasts before it wears out (according to the actual useful lives of the equipment that different industries use), some industries are taxed far more lightly than others.

The accompanying table shows what the likely corporate tax will be on the income from a typical investment in different industries. Although the corporate tax rate in the law is 46 percent, every industry would pay less than 46 percent in tax over the lifetime of its investments, because the depreciation deductions in the current tax law are overly accelerated and thus reduce the tax paid. The overall effective tax rate for some of these industries will be even higher when income from other capital assets is taken into account. For example, the effective tax rate for services and trade is close to 30 percent. But even more troublesome from an economic efficiency point of view are the tremendous differences in tax rates among industries—ranging from 12 percent for oil extraction to 30 percent for trade. The problem is that the low tax rates in the oil industry (and other lightly taxed industries such as construction and communications) will attract investment away from the highly taxed industries. Even if the marketplace says that we need more investment in trade, services, or manufacturing by allowing those industries a higher pretax rate of return, investment would tend to flow toward the more lightly taxed sectors because the tax advantages are so great.

This is not to say that there is anything wrong with the oil industry, or that we need to be swimming in retail stores. But we are competing in a rapidly changing world economy. When the marketplace signals that there is an investment opportunity in some particular sector by offering a high rate of return, we can't have the tax system standing in the way—or some other nation will get there first. And because we don't know where those opportunities will turn up, we can only accept a tax system that taxes all industries the same, so that the opportunities that the marketplace offers before taxes will also be the most attractive after taxes.

Table 4.1 *Tax Rates on Typical Investments in Different Industries*

Industry	Tax Rate
Agriculture	25%
Mining	19
Oil Extraction	12
Construction	13
Manufacturing	29
Transportation	19
Communications	16
Radio and TV	19
Electric and Gas	25
Trade	30
Services	29

Source: Gregg A. Esenwein and Jane Gravelle, *Effective Tax Rates Under the Accelerated Cost Recovery System (ACRS) and the Tax Equity and Fiscal Responsibility Act of 1982 (TEFRA)*, (Congressional Research Service, Library of Congress, 3 January 1983).

An executive of a large multinational conglomerate told me in the depths of the 1982 recession that he was simply liquidating high-tax companies, buying low-tax, low-debt companies, gutting them, and moving on with a solid balance sheet. The longer-term future of those companies and workers that provided his bridge over the recession was of no interest to the fast-moving executive who eighteen months later had himself moved on to another company, where he would undoubtedly make the same short-term decisions and take the money and run. Such manipulation, invited by the disparity in effective corporate tax rates, hurts our efforts to keep America number one. It is a practice not followed by most of our responsible corporate giants, *but it should be followed by none.*

These big tax breaks caused even more trouble—the usual problem of leakage of tax incentives. Lots of sharp tax-shelter operators quickly saw that the tax breaks were so big that investments didn't have to *earn* money to *make* money. Since the Reagan tax cuts, tax shelters have been booming. Want to buy a few llamas? If you are in the top tax bracket, a "creative tax planner" will be glad to tell you how it will make you money—by reducing your taxes, of course. If llamas are too exotic for you, racehorses or even plain old cows will do. Or if you are into the arts, master recordings of phonograph records, master plates of collector postage stamps, or old books might be just right. Needless to say, none of these "investments" is going to do much for our productivity or competitiveness. But they will benefit handsomely from the business tax loopholes.

Besides the problems of depreciation and the investment tax credit, there is an array of loopholes in the corporate tax code. Among the most prominent are special tax breaks for particular industries. Oil gets percentage depletion and expensing of intangible drilling costs; timber gets the capital gains exclusion for cut trees. These loopholes make both of these industries favorites with tax-shelter promoters. Banks get a special deduction for prospective losses on bad debts, even if they never have to write off a loan; and so banks pay only the tiniest fraction of their net income in tax.

All of these loopholes are so valuable because we have a high tax rate–high subsidy system. For large corporations with more than $100,000 in profits, the tax is virtually a straight 46 percent of taxable income. So any tax deduction for corporations saves 46 cents on the dollar. It is no wonder that the "three-martini lunch" is such a popular corporate perk. It is a chance for the corporation to make its employees happy, at just about half price—after taxes.

The Fair Tax addresses these problems in much the same way as it attacks the high tax-rate problems in the individual income tax: by closing the loopholes and lowering the rates. The Fair Tax slows the depreciation of business buildings and machinery to a rate that allows an adequate cushion for inflation somewhat more rapid than we are experiencing today (about 7 percent), and it repeals the investment tax credit. Many other corporate tax loopholes are repealed. Then the corporate tax rate is lowered to a straight 30 percent. The Fair Tax is not a tax cut for corporations, nor does it soak corporations. It will collect the same revenues as under current law.

The lower 30 percent rate does two very positive things for the economy and the tax system. First, it is a tremendous incentive to investment and productivity. Under the current tax law, a corporation might enjoy the big tax benefits for a new investment, but if the investment really pays off, the profits are taxed at the very high 46 percent corporate rate. Under the Fair Tax, with its 30 percent rate, there is a greater incentive to seek the investments that yield the big payoffs—and make the economy more productive and efficient.

Second, because the value of a corporate tax deduction is less, at 30 cents on the dollar, there is much less of an incentive to play the tax deductions to the hilt. Corporate executives will not spend all fall deciding how to roll over investments so as to lower their taxes. Instead, they will spend time making more money. If a firm thinks that it is productive to send an employee out for a business lunch—and it can be—that is fine. But the firm had better think carefully, because it is paying 70 percent of the price after the tax deduction, not 54 percent. The same is true of automobiles or any other business expenditure. The low tax rate is the best incentive because it can't be "gamed." You can fake an investment by buying a llama, but you can't—and wouldn't *want* to—fake taxable income to take advantage of a low tax rate.

Under the Fair Tax, industries like petroleum, timber, and banking will be treated fairly—no better than others, but no worse. Tax-shelter opportunities will be much reduced, and investors will find it more profitable to put their money into growing, productive firms than into tax gimmicks. That is what the economy needs.

A square deal with the tax law, it turns out, will be a big improvement for some of the most dynamic firms in the economy. The high-tech sector is heavily taxed, largely because those firms have not yet obtained their own special tax breaks, as more established industries have. We could give these firms their own tax break—but that would reduce government revenue and take only one sector off the list of industries that are disadvantaged by the current system. Instead, by setting up a low-rate, loophole-free tax system, we not only remove the biases against the high-tech firms, but we establish the incentives to nurture the *next* growth sector, whatever it may be.

The Fair Tax also gives lower tax rates to, among others, the retail and food and fiber industries, which account for more than 40 million jobs in America. Small businesses, particularly those organized as partnerships, will benefit from the reduced individual income tax rates.

Finally, notice that the 30 percent corporate tax rate is precisely equal to the highest individual income tax rate. This eliminates an incentive to create "personal service corporations" that play on the tax-rate differences between corporations and individuals to avoid taxes. Personal service corporations are widely used by professionals such as doctors and lawyers—and professional basketball players.

So the Fair Tax cleans up the corporate income tax, just as it does the individual income tax. With fewer loopholes and lower tax rates, it shifts the emphasis from tax minimization to profit and progress. If we put more of our energy into building better products instead of dodging the IRS, our corporations will win battles in the marketplace, and not just in Tax Court.

CONCLUSION

So the Fair Tax isn't a free lunch. We can't give away big tax cuts and pretend that it won't cause deficits; that has been tried, and it doesn't work. That was the lesson of the 1981 Tax Bill. We can't cut tax rates without closing loopholes. That was the lesson of the 1982 Tax Bill.

A tax system with lower rates and fewer preferential tax provisions is much fairer than the current system, and a tax system that allows fewer tax shelters, with more taxpayers bearing their fair share, is more worthy of respect. After all, if the federal government cannot set fair standards in taxation, how can it uphold justice in other aspects of our national life?

The Fair Tax bears no hidden agenda. It is all in the open for everyone to see. It holds constant the relative tax liabilities of income groups and corporations. Finally, with its low tax rates, the Fair Tax is open to the dynamism of the U.S. economy. It *encourages* change—because an innovator need not overcome any tax advantages of established ways of doing things. So the Fair Tax is fairer, simpler, and more efficient than the current tax law. As such, it is better for the economy, and better for the country.

5 The Fair and Simple Tax (FAST)

Jack Kemp

The case against the current corporate and personal income tax system is overwhelming and devastating. Few have ever come forward in its defense. The system fails, and fails miserably, on the traditional public finance criteria: equity, efficiency, and simplicity. It is a monstrous system that cries out for major overhaul. Piecemeal reform will only paint over a foundation that is cracked and flawed to its core.

We need a tax system that is simple, throwing away the thousands of pages of complex and unneeded rules, regulations, and red tape—a system in which taxpayers clearly know their obligations and can figure out their taxes without the help of fancy accountants and lawyers. We need a tax system that is fair, one that assures working taxpayers that all Americans will pay their fair share and not skip out of paying taxes by crawling through loopholes. Fairness means that taxes should be proportional to the ability to pay. We need a tax code that rewards enterprise, initiative, and thrift. Only if the tax code improves incentives for productive activities will the economy flourish as jobs are created and poverty reduced.

This chapter is adapted from the author's prepared statement for the Treasury Tax Reform and Simplification Study Hearings, July 1984 (proc.).

AN OVERVIEW

The Kemp-Kasten bill incorporates these principles. It will not solve all the problems of the current tax code, but it certainly goes a long way. We are willing to make further modifications to the bill as necessary and prudent. Kemp-Kasten incorporates the following salient features:

1. FAST cuts the top marginal tax rate in half, dropping it down from 50 percent to 25 percent. After deducting generous personal allowances and a new employment-income exclusion, all taxable income is taxed at the same 25 percent tax rate.

2. FAST helps poor people by lifting the income tax threshold above the poverty line and thereby removing a million and a half of the poorest Americans from the tax roles. FAST indexes the tax code and thereby halts bracket creep—the unfairest tax of all on the poor.

3. FAST is fair to low- and middle-income taxpayers. Many flat-rate tax plans raise average taxes on lower- and middle-income taxpayers. But FAST excludes from taxes one-fifth of a family's employment income up to about the $40,000 income level to protect wage and salary earners. The exclusion is phased out entirely at about $100,000. This exclusion lowers the effective and marginal income tax rates on low- and middle-income Americans and helps offset the Social Security payroll tax, resulting in a smooth, almost flat total tax rate.

4. FAST simplifies the tax code. It broadens the tax base by eliminating most tax preferences or "loopholes." However, important deductions are retained for interest (including mortgages), charitable contributions, real property taxes, and catastrophic medical expenses. Also retained are the current tax treatment of IRAs, Keoghs, and Social Security and veterans' benefits.

5. FAST helps families. The tax code has penalized families and children because the dependent exemption has not kept up with inflation. FAST doubles the personal exemption (and indexes it to keep pace with inflation),

increases (and indexes) the zero-bracket amount, and provides a generous employment exclusion—all of which provides important protection for working families.

6. FAST indexes the tax code to protect everyone from future tax increases caused by inflation. For the first time, capital gains are indexed for inflation, to end the taxation of phony, inflated "gains" on assets like stocks or houses. For the first ten years, taxpayers may choose an exclusion of 25 percent instead of indexation.

7. FAST improves the corporate tax code. Most tax preferences are repealed and the marginal tax rate is cut from 46 percent to 30 percent, with a reduced 15 percent rate for small businesses. The new depreciation schedules enacted in 1981 are retained, and the corporate capital gains tax is also reduced from 28 percent to 20 percent. Expensing for small business is also retained.

8. FAST raises roughly the same tax revenues as now on a static basis. FAST also keeps about the same distribution of tax burden on various income groups as the current tax system. Those taxpayers who use tax preferences less than average would receive a tax cut. For example, a family of four earning $20,000 that does not itemize deductions would receive a tax cut of $616.

The Personal Income Tax

FAST combines fairness with sound economic theory. And it is simple, eliminating most deductions and special provisions that have encrusted our tax system. For most taxpayers, their FAST tax return could fit on one piece of paper.

FAST is also fair. Three features of the FAST proposal combine to increase the income tax threshhold at which taxpayers begin to pay federal income tax: the double personal exemption, the increase in zero-bracket amounts (standard deductions), and the new exclusion for employment income. As a result of these generous allowances, Americans near or below the poverty level would no longer pay income tax under FAST. The income at which people start paying income tax would rise from $3,445 to $5,875 for a single taxpayer, and from $8,936 to $14,375 for a family of four. What is just as important, the FAST plan makes sure that his protections will always exist in the future. Under FAST, the personal exemption, the zero-bracket amounts, and the employment-income exclusion are all indexed to keep up with inflation.

FAST helps millions more escape from the poverty, retirement, and unemployment "traps," caused by a combination of high tax rates and the reduction in social-welfare payments as income rises. FAST allows the retired, poor, and low-income unemployed to keep more of their earnings as they enter the work force. This not only restores incentive to seek work rather than rely totally on government benefits, but it provides these low-income groups with greater means to dig themselves out of poverty.

The Employment-Income Exclusion

A distinctive feature of the Kemp-Kasten "Fair and Simple Tax" is a new "up-front" or "above-the-line" exclusion for part of wages and salaries: the employment-income exclusion. In general, taxpayers may exclude 20 percent of wage and salary income up to the Social Security wage base (which is $39,300 in 1985 and indexed by law). Above that point, the maximum exclusion is reduced by 12.5 percent of a taxpayer's wages and salary in excess of the Social Security wage base. For 1985 this results in a zero exclusion for all incomes larger than $102,180.

Two exceptions are permitted for the sake of fairness. First, single taxpayers with less than $10,000 in wages and salaries ($20,000 for joint returns) may exclude 20 percent of all gross income up to $10,000 ($20,000 for joint returns). This especially helps retired senior citizens. Second, two-earner couples with combined wages and salaries in excess of the Social Security wage base may figure their exclusions separately and add the two.

This provision has several advantages. First, it protects the poorest individuals and families, by raising the threshold at which they start paying income tax. Second, for middle-income taxpayers, the exclusion offsets most of the Social Security payroll tax rate. Without such a provision, a flat income tax rate would result in significantly higher combined marginal tax rates (Social Security plus income tax), below the Social Security wage base rather than above it. The FAST plan fixes the problem. (The marginal tax rate is the tax on an additional dollar of income.)

Third, the exclusion results in smooth, virtually flat total marginal tax rates both below and above the Social Security wage base. It keeps the tax rates on employment and savings income about the same above the income tax threshold. And compared with a "pure" flat income tax, the exclusion reduces the tax burden for all wages and salaries less than about $100,000. Incomes larger than about $100,000 receive no benefit from the exclusion. Finally, the employment-income exclusion helps keep the distribution of the income tax burden virtually unchanged in each income class, right up to the point at which the exclusion disppears. This makes FAST fairer than a straight flat-rate tax, while remaining almost as simple.

Marginal Tax Rates

Undoubtedly, FAST's most important feature is its low marginal tax rates, which encourages upward mobility, thrift, and enterprise. FAST cuts today's top marginal tax rate in half, from 50 percent to 25 percent. This increases after-tax incentives by up to one-half. Taxpayers will no longer be rewarded for investing in boxcars, paper transactions, and tax scams. With tax rates up to 50 percent, every dollar of tax deduction is worth 50 cents. But at 25 percent tax rates, most tax shelters and deductions would not be profitable. Few would pay 30 or 40 cents on every dollar for a tax shelter, as many now do, to save 25 cents in taxes.

A low marginal tax rate also lowers the cost of labor while increasing its reward. It minimizes the "tax wedge," which is the difference between a worker's after-tax wage and his cost to his firm. A worker considers his "reward" for working his after-tax wage, net of all deductions and taxes. He will work harder the greater his after-tax pay. An employer, however, is interested in the worker's cost to his firm, which includes payroll taxes, state and local taxes, and payroll deductions. The greater the gross wage of each additional worker, the fewer workers the firm can afford to hire.

An auto firm now must give a typical worker $1.45 per hour to provide a $1 raise after payroll and federal, state, and local income taxes. The 45-cent tax wedge, most economists believe, imposes a cost on the economy far in excess of the tax revenue raised. The tax wedge in the labor markets reduces the demand for workers—creating unemployment—and lowers the reward for working, both of which reduce the economy's potential output.

Taxes on interest income also drive a wedge between the after-tax return to saving, which is the reward that savers receive for foregoing consumption, and the real benefit of savings to society represented by the pretax interest rate. The tax wedge reduces the incentive to save, driving down the level of saving; it also increases the cost of funds, thus reducing investment.

In the FAST tax, average tax rates remain approximately what they are now. But marginal taxes are cut dramatically—reducing the tax wedge distorting the leisure-labor and the savings-consumption choice. FAST will encourage additional employment, since the cost of labor is reduced, and will increase the supply of workers, since the reward for working is enhanced. It will generate more saving by increasing the after-tax return, and it will increase the demand for saving by increasing the rate of return on investment. But the level and combination of labor and capital will be more efficient under FAST. The economy's potential output, employment rate, and efficiency all will be bolstered.

Corporate Income Tax

Kemp-Kasten also brings some sanity into the corporate income tax. FAST rewards profit by taxing it at the lowest possible marginal tax rate. And it puts an end to many tax-avoidance schemers, loophole exploiters, and paper shufflers.

FAST reduces the wide disparity in tax rates between investments and among industries. FAST eliminates the investment tax credit and lowers marginal tax rates to end the equipment tax subsidy and create a much more consistent range of tax rates for new investment. At 4 percent inflation, the range of tax rates under FAST would vary only between 20 and 31 percent.

FAST's effective tax rates on new investment are slightly higher than the current system on some asset classes and slightly lower on others; FAST modestly increases overall effective corporate tax rates on new investment. FAST, however, reduces corporate income tax rates on existing assets by one-third. Lower corporate rates encourage more efficient and productive use of assets—both labor and capital. The investment tax credit, which in some cases subsidizes the purchase of new equipment, sometimes causes a churning of assets simply to generate a one-time tax advantage.

FAST will also be more fair to labor-intensive firms. Many businesses were not able to use many of the 1981 capital-cost-recovery provisions either because they had insufficient income or were not capital-intensive. As such, they have faced much higher effective tax rates. But why should firms that are innovative, growing, and profitable have to pay much higher rax rates than other industries? Under FAST, the top tax rate will be cut to 30 percent, creating a greater incentive for firms to invest in new projects, regardless of their labor-capital mix. FAST promotes a more neutral tax system that doesn't subsidize or target any industry and minimizes interference in the free market.

FAST also improves the corporate tax system and ameliorates distortions in the following ways:

1. The reduction in the corporate rate from 46 to 30 percent helps small corporations that typically cannot use the capital-cost-recovery provisions as much as many larger businesses. Small family-owned businesses that usually pay taxes through individual income tax schedules benefit from the reduction in the top individual income tax rate from 50 to 25 percent.

2. Kemp-Kasten reduces the bias favoring debt financing. At a 30 percent corporate rate, $1 of interest deduction reduces the corporate tax bill by 30 cents, while at the current 46 percent corporate tax rate, $1 of interest expense is worth 46 cents in tax reduction. Kemp-Kasten reduces the relative advantage of debt-over-equity financing by one-third.

3. FAST significantly reduces the double taxation of corporate income. The bill cuts the corporate profits tax (from 46 to 30 percent) and also the top marginal tax rate on dividends (from 50 to 25 percent) and capital gains (from 20 to 18.75 percent). Under the current system, corporate capital could be taxed at combined tax rates up to 73 percent. Under Kemp-Kasten, corporate income will be taxed at combined rates up to only 48 percent, reducing the total tax rate on corporate capital by up to one-third.

Tax Distribution

Kemp-Kasten is revenue-neutral, within a few percentage points, for every income class below $100,000, according to a preliminary analysis by the Joint Committee on Taxation (JCT). For income groups over $100,000, the preliminary figures show static tax cuts averaging about

20 percent. These figures are incomplete, since the JCT has not included in its model many of the tax preferences we repeal. These so-called off-budget items total about $10 billion and are believed by the JCT to affect upper-income taxpayers disproportionately. Including these preferences, the static revenue loss from higher-income groups should be around 15 percent. I believe we will approach revenue neutrality in the upper income categories when the incentive effects of the tax rate reductions are taken into account.

Revenue Consequences

Kemp-Kasten is rougly revenue-neutral. Based on 1981 income levels, the JCT has estimated that Kemp-Kasten would raise about 97 percent of the income tax revenue actually raised that year assuming it does not increase income through improved incentives.

CONCLUSION

The current tax system requires radical reform. Piecemeal changes will neither solve the monstrous problems of the current system nor overcome the political challenges of the special interests that stand behind every tax break. Trying to change one provision or another in isolation will fail, thwarted by entrenched special interests. Tinkering will not simplify the tax code, restore simplicity and fairness, create jobs, or spur economic growth.

We need to change the tax system in one bold stroke. This will disarm special interests and gather broad public support. Even those who may lose one loophole or another will support a reform that promises a larger economic pie. The Kemp-Kasten bill is economically and politically viable. It recognizes that the tax system is unfair, riddled with loopholes, and harsh on the poor. It also recognizes that high marginal tax rates damage economic growth. And it answers the worry of working taxpayers that single-rate taxes mean higher taxes. I hope that we can join with House members on both sides of the aisle, in a nonpartisan initiative, to give the American people a tax code that is fair and simple for everyone.

6 A Cash Flow Tax System

Henry J. Aaron
Harvey Galper

The proposal advanced for a cash flow tax system is based on the premise that a greater degree of fairness, economic efficiency, and administrative simplicity can be achieved by establishing a consistent expenditure or cash flow tax than by trying to establish a consistent income tax. We recognize that the real world is too complex and varied to permit genuine simplicity in taxation and that all practical taxes involve some distortions and unfairness. But we believe this proposal would be a substantial improvement over the present system.

THE TAX ON INDIVIDUALS

We propose that persons be taxed at the household level (as at present), but on their cash flow, not on their income. Each taxpaying unit would be taxed on all cash receipts, minus net saving. Both receipts and savings would be comprehensively defined. Receipts would include all wages and salaries, rent, interest, profits, dividends, transfer payments, gifts received, and inheritances. Savings would include all net payments into certain "qualified accounts," including all financial assets (stocks, bonds, and other securities), all accounts in banks and

---

This chapter is from *Economic Choices*, Alice M. Rivlin, ed. (Brookings Institution, 1984), pp. 93–100.

other depository institutions, the cash value of life insurance, and real estate (except owner-occupied housing).

Just as additions to saving would be deducted from income, such dissaving as the sale of stock or withdrawal from a bank account would be added to the tax base. Similarly, the proceeds from loans would be included in the tax base, and loan repayments, including both principal and interest, would be deducted from receipts in calculating the tax base.

Inheritances would be counted as a receipt, but if they were not consumed, they would be exactly offset by an increase in savings. Gifts and bequests would be treated as spending in the year in which they were made, subject to an averaging provision if the amounts transferred were large relative to annual cash flow.

It would be desirable to award each person a lifetime exemption for making a certain amount of gifts or bequests in order to permit tax-free transfers, such as those between parents and children, at time of need. A lifetime exemption of $100,000 per person ($200,000 per couple) would permit most families to exclude all gifts and bequests from tax. Under the cash flow tax, taxation of gifts and bequests over the exemption amount would be a substitute for current taxation under the federal estate and gift tax, which could then be repealed. The inclusion of both inheritances and bequests in the cash flow tax base is essential to fulfill the principle of fairness in taxation. If they are included, the cash flow tax base would correctly measure resources available to each person over his or her lifetime.

Personal exemptions would be allowed as under the present personal income tax, although the amount should be modified. We propose as a minimum standard that no tax be imposed on persons whose consumption is less than current poverty thresholds. Based on estimates for 1984, tax-free levels of consumption would be set at $5,000 for a single person, $8,250 for couples, and $1,500 for each additional dependent. In addition, some account should be taken of the fact that one-earner families are better off than two-earner families with the same income. Two-earner families lose in-home services provided by the nonearning spouse in a one-earner household and may incur money costs for child care and other household services. Accordingly, we recommend the continued deduction of 10 percent of the earnings of the spouse with lesser earnings, up to some maximum level (the limit under current law is $30,000 per year). This deduction would have the effect of increasing tax-free levels of consumption for two-earner families. Similarly, a credit for low earners, like the earned-income tax credit now allowed certain workers with low earnings, might be provided.

Tax rates would be progressive under the cash flow tax. Because the base for the cash flow tax is broader than that for the current personal income tax, the same revenues could be raised with lower rates. For joint returns, existing revenues could be matched with a 5 percent tax on the first $10,000 of taxable expenditures, 20 percent on the next $30,000 of taxable expenditures, and 32 percent on taxable expenditures over $40,000 per year. For single persons, the same rates would apply to taxable expenditure brackets of 0 to $5,000, $5,000 to $40,000, and over $40,000. To raise the additional revenue needed to balance the budget in fiscal year 1989, these rates would have to become 6 percent, 24 percent, and 38 percent. These rates would apply only to expenditures above tax-free ranges, defined by the enlarged personal exemptions and increased zero-bracket amounts. These rates would approximately reproduce the distribution of tax burdens under the current personal income tax, except for reductions in taxes among low-income taxpayers, who would benefit from the increased tax-free ranges. For example, a four-person family would pay no tax on up to $11,250 of expenditures per year; in contrast, that same family is taxable under current law on income over $7,400 per year.

Because bequests would be included in the cash flow tax base (subject to averaging), burdens on taxpayers would be reduced throughout their working years and increased substantially at death. The main reason why taxation at death would be increased is that the cash flow tax on bequests would be designed to be harder to avoid than the present estate tax.

If no changes were made in the income tax base, the revenue targets could be met by increasing current rates, which range from 11 percent to 50 percent, to 13 to 59 percent. In contrast, the cash flow tax could meet these targets with rates ranging from 6 percent to 38 percent.

Except for personal exemptions, a working-spouse deduction, and the special deductions for limited amounts of wealth transfers, any further deductions, credits, or exclusions would represent a step away from the principles of fairness and efficiency. We recognize that rigorous adherence to this principle would terminate some of the most important and popular advantages conferred on particular sources or uses of income by the present tax laws. For example, all transfer payments would be potentially taxable; wealth would be taxed in full when consumed or transferred to another person; home mortgage interest would no longer be deductible; and deductions for state and local taxes would be disallowed. The relative tax advantage that state and local governments enjoy because interest on debt is exempt from federal tax would also end, since all capital income would be included in the tax base in full unless it was saved.

The pressure would be strong to retain many of these concessions, and a few should probably be retained. But it is vital to recognize that these and other special provisions bear much of the responsibility for the complexity, unfairness, and inefficency of the present system. Moreover, each attempt to exempt a source or use of income from the tax base means that the tax rates would have to be raised to generate the same amount of revenue from the lower base.

THE TAX ON BUSINESS

Recent tax legislation has lowered the effective rate of corporate taxation, albeit erratically, and reduced the-corporate tax to a minor source of federal revenue (about 10 percent of the total in fiscal year 1984).

Scrapping the corporate tax altogether and taxing the income generated by corporations only when it is paid out to individuals is an idea that has some appeal. Unfortunately, scrapping the corporate tax would raise three serious problems. First, the increasing amount of U.S. business income flowing to foreigners would escape taxation. Second, individuals would use the corporate form to avoid taxation. Corporations would be able to finance tax-free consumption for employees and stockholders by purchasing a wide variety of consumption goods, such as automobiles, housing, life insurance, health care, or legal services—indeed, almost anything. Third, repeal of the corporate income tax would represent a windfall gain for corporate owners of depreciable capital. For these reasons, the corporate tax should be retained. But it should be reformed to make it neutral with respect to different types of investments and to discourage its use to avoid the personal cash flow tax.

The corporate tax we propose would have two parts. The first would be a tax on the cash flow of corporations. The corporation tax base would include total receipts of the corporation from all sources other than the sale of stock, less all business expenses, including investment. Deductions for business expenditures on consumption items for the benefit of employees or owners would be denied. Deductions for consumption expenditures by noncorporate businesses would also be denied. The business tax base would include the proceeds from borrowing. Corporations would be entitled to deduct all debt-service payments, but no deductions would be permitted for dividends or any other cash distribution to stockholders. The exclusion of both the proceeds from sale of stock and of dividends has the effect of exempting returns equal to the government's borrowing rate from tax at the business level.

If firms borrowed to finance investment, no tax would result in the year the investment was made; the expenditure on the investment would just offset the proceeds from the loan. If earnings on the investment differed from the repayment of debt, corporate cash flow and tax liabilities would be affected. The same principles would be applied to the cash flow of noncorporate businesses. In particular, new investments and debt transactions would be treated in the same way. Net cash flow, however, would be included immediately in the tax base of the owners, although there would be an offsetting deduction for saving if the funds remained in the business or were saved.

The second element of the tax on corporations would be a withholding tax on all distributions from corporations to foreign individuals and corporations. This tax would apply to dividends, interest, rents, royalties, proceeds from liquidation, or any other cash distribution.

The corporate cash flow tax would complement the individual cash flow tax and would have major advantages over the present corporation income tax. It would do away with the need to engage in complex accounting for depreciation, since investment would be treated as a deductible expense at the time it is made. It would avoid other inflation-related distortions in the definition of business income. It would avoid the complexities of defining long-term capital gains and the avenues for tax avoidance that this favored source of income creates. The cash flow tax would continue to impose tax on the income from capital in existence when the new system was adopted. In addition, it would minimize use of corporations to avoid the individual spending tax. The withholding tax would fall on payments abroad that are generated in the United States. The rate of the corporate cash flow tax would equal the maximum rate on personal cash flow.

These proposals would cause major changes in the U.S. tax system and would have far-reaching effects. But the tax system is so riddled with ad hoc and contradictory rules entrenched in past personal and business decisions that any effort to establish a consistent and fair system will have similarly wrenching effects. For this reason, care is needed in devising adequate transition rules and in dealing with special circumstances. The treatment of housing, education, and international capital and investment flows, for example, requires particular attention.

But these problems should not prevent action on tax reform. The consequence of failure to act will be the perpetuation of unfairness, inefficiency, and complexity. The gains in these areas would fully justify the inevitable problems associated with transition. The United States must begin now to reform its tax system.

7 A Simple Income Tax with Low Marginal Rates

Robert E. Hall
Alvin Rabushka

Despite recent progress in lowering income tax rates, the American tax system is in disgrace, in dire need of simplification and reform. It is inordinately lengthy, filling volumes of the tax code, and is complicated by hundreds of credits, exemptions, and special provisions. Many taxpayers require expensive professional help to fill out their tax returns correctly. Each act of Congress further complicates the system, and political promises of real simplification and reform of the tax system remain unfulfilled.

The tax system consists chiefly of the personal income tax, the corporate income tax, and the Social Security payroll tax. The personal income tax has steeply progressive rates, rising to a maximum marginal rate of 50 percent under the new tax law. The income base to which these progressive rates are applied has steadily eroded over the years through a wide variety of exclusions,

---

This chapter is based on the authors' *The Flat Rate Tax*, Hearings Before the Subcommittee on Monetary and Fiscal Policy of the Joint Economic Committee, 97th Congress, 2d sess., 27 July and 19 August 1982, as modified by their testimony before the Committee on Ways and Means, House of Representatives, 26 September 1984.

deductions, and exemptions to the point where it now constitutes no more than half of the total national income. The personal income tax discourages savings. Income is first taxed when earned and again when savings earn interest. Even worse, the returns to savings put into the corporate sector are taxed twice, once as corporate profits and again at the household level when dividends are paid. A growing chorus of criticism contends that the current system attenuates individual incentives to work, save, and invest. For many taxpayers, saving a dollar in taxes is worth twice as much as earning another dollar in income.

Prior to the twentieth century, federal revenues, comprising about 3 percent of the GNP, were largely collected from customs duties. With the adoption of the Sixteenth Amendment in 1913 and the payroll tax in the 1930s, federal revenues have grown to consume 22 percent of the GNP. Escalating inflation in the 1970s pushed growing numbers of taxpayers into high tax brackets that twenty years ago were meant only for the very rich. Costly side effects have begun to surface.

Scholarly research, along with Internal Revenue Service reports, reveals widespread evidence of tax evasion on interest, dividend, and other forms of household or professional income. Tax shelters are now a commonplace feature of the financial landscape. Estimates of the underground economy range from several tens of billions to several hundred billion dollars. In the eighteenth century, customs duties exceeding 100 percent made England into a nation of smugglers. Today, marginal tax rates of 50 percent from the personal income tax, 46 percent from the corporate tax, and 14 percent from the payroll tax are converting Americans into tax evaders as they channel their investments into tax shelters. The current system fosters contempt for the law and simultaneously discourages productive economic activity.

Why is the tax system so difficult to reform? Most scholars and lawmakers routinely claim that it is politically infeasible to reform radically the tax system. Talk of simplification is a sign of unrealism. Congress would, it is alleged, never abolish the exemptions and deductions for mortgage interest payments, charitable contributions, and excess medical costs or remove the many benefits and credits enjoyed by low-income households and a bevy of special-interest groups. The American demand for justice means that the rich should pay higher taxes. As a result, changes in the tax code are incremental and represent only slight modifications to the corporate or personal income tax.

We sense growing interest on the part of the public and in Congress for a drastic reform of the tax system. As a contribution to the debate and discussion on this important subject, we propose a simple income tax based on low marginal rates to replace the entire current system of separate tax-rate schedules on corporate and individual income. The new tax would be a low, flat rate that would apply to all taxpayers, excluding the very poor, and to all types of income. It is based on a much larger tax base than the present system and thus would generate similar amounts of revenue as the current high-rate system with its exemptions and deductions. The simple flat rate would end "bracket creep," which is caused by inflation pushing people into higher tax brackets. It would largely minimize the marriage penalty that current law imposes on two-earner households. It would be stable, predictable, and cease further proliferation of a variety of tax credits used to attain social goals. Most important, it would restore the incentives to work, save, and invest, thereby promoting growth and higher standards of living.

Our proposal does not include reform of the Social Security payroll tax and the retirement benefits it finances, although reform is long overdue. The Social Security tax cannot be discussed separately from benefits, and we would be taken too far from the subject of income tax reform to catalogue the massive changes in Social Security that are needed to put the system on a sound footing.

BASIC PRINCIPLES OF THE SIMPLE INCOME TAX

The simple income tax rests on four basic principles:

1. All income should be taxed only once, as close as possible to its source.
2. All types of income should be taxed at the same low rate.
3. The poorest households should pay no income tax.
4. Tax returns for both households and businesses should be simple enough to fit on a postcard or on a one-page form.

We propose the replacement of the existing corporate and personal income taxes with a business tax and a compensation tax. The business tax includes rental income and the earnings of corporations, unincorporated businesses, farms, and professionals. The business tax does not permit a deduction for interest payments, dividends, or other payments to the owners of the business. As a result, all income that individuals receive from business activity has already been taxed and should not be taxed again. The same rule applies to capital gains. The business tax is like a withholding tax; it means that the IRS does not have to track down all the interest, dividends, capital gains, and other business income received by the public. Compensation would be the only element of household income not taxed under the business tax. We propose a new compensation tax to replace the present personal income tax. The compensation tax would have a set of personal allowances to ensure that the poorest families pay no compensation tax.

Under existing law, tax rates can be as high as 50 percent for compensation and 80 percent for business income, because income is taxed first under the corporate tax and again under the personal tax. To collect the same amount of revenue that the present system generates, assuming the same flows of income, the simple tax system would require a standard rate of only 19 percent.

THE BUSINESS TAX

The new business tax would rationalize the present hodgepodge of federal tax provisions for business income. It would reduce the high marginal rates currently paid on some types of income from capital. By eliminating interest deductions, it would also end the subsidies embodied in current tax shelters. A uniform rate of 19 percent would replace the current range of tax rates, which stretches from actual subsidy of highly leveraged tax shelters with large interest deductions to rates as high as 80 percent imposed on income earned by corporate stockholders.

The new business tax applies equally to all forms of business—corporate, partnership, professional, farm, rentals, and royalties. The base for the tax is gross revenue less purchases of goods and services and compensation paid to employees. In addition, a capital-recovery allowance is deducted for investment in plant and equipment. No deductions for depreciation, interest, or payments to owners are permitted. However, the self-employed may pay themselves salary in any amount they choose, provided they report it on the compensation tax form.

The business tax return would fit easily on a single page, even for a multibillion-dollar corporation (Fig. 7.1). Gross revenue from sales does not include earnings the business may receive from its ownership of other businesses (provided these businesses file their own tax returns) or from its ownership of securities. These earnings have already been taxed in other businesses. Gross revenue does include sales of used plant and equipment. Businesses are not required to maintain inventory or depreciation accounts for tax purposes.

In place of the myriad investment incentives in the current tax system, we propose the use of straightforward

Figure 7.1 *Hall-Rubushka Simplified Flat-Rate Tax Form*

Form 2	Business Tax	1985
Business Name		Employer Identification #
Street Address		County
City, State and ZIP Code		Principal Product

1 Gross revenue from sales	1	
2 Allowable costs		
(*a*) Purchases of goods, services and materials	2(a)	
(*b*) Wages, salaries and pensions	2(b)	
(*c*) Purchases of capital equipment, structures, and land	2(c)	
3 Total allowable costs *(sum of lines 2(a), 2(b), 2(c))*	3	
4 Taxable income *(line 1 less line 3)*	4	
5 Tax *(19% of line 4)*	5	
6 Carry-forward from 1984	6	
7 Interest on carry-forward *(10% of line 6)*	7	
8 Carry-forward into 1985 *(line 6 plus line 7)*	8	
9 Tax due *(line 5 less line 8, if positive)*	9	
10 Carry-forward to 1986 *(line 8 less line 5, if positive)*	10	

first-year write-off of all business investment, both in new and used plant and equipment. First-year capital recovery is a great simplification over the complicated depreciation deductions and investment credits allowed under present tax law. It also eliminates the present problem that depreciation based on historical cost is not rapid enough to offset the effects of inflation. The first-year system avoids all distortions of inflation.

In 1981 the net revenue of U.S. business was $1,179 billion. Under the new business tax, capital recovery allowances would have been $349 billion, leaving net taxable business income at $830 billion. A tax rate of 19 percent would have yielded $158 billion, nearly triple the revenue from the actual corporate income tax in 1981 or $57 billion. The extra revenue, despite the much lower tax rate, comes from (1) the much wider tax base, including unincorporated business, and (2) taxing business income at its source.

Under the simple tax system, all business income would be taxed only once—at its source. Household receipts of interst, dividends, and capital gains would be considered after-tax income. Although wealthy households might receive large amounts of these types of income, it is important to understand that the taxes on this income have already been paid. The recipient household itself should not pay any more tax on business income. Taxing business income at its source has an important practical benefit. Under the present personal income tax, large amounts of interest and dividend income escape taxation through outright tax evasion and avoidance. Under our business tax, the only way dividends, interest, and other earnings of capital could escape taxation would be for the business to fail to file a tax return, which is easier to detect and punish than tax evasion.

Capital gains on rental property, plant, and equipment are taxed under the business tax. The purchase price is deducted at the time of purchase, and the sale price is taxed at the time of the sale. These provisions are most important for real estate, where they will eliminate the current abuses in which low capital-gains tax rates create an incentive for artificial turnover of property. Every owner of rental real estate would be required to fill out the simple business tax return.

Capital gains in the overall value of a successful firm are also taxed under the new business tax and should not be taxed again at the household level. Consider the case of the common stock of a corporation. The value of its stock in the market is the capitalization of its future earnings. Because the owners of the stock receive the earnings after the corporation has paid the business tax, that tax depresses the stock's market value. When future earnings rise, the stock rises in value and its owners receive capital gains. When the high earnings materialize in the future, they will be correspondingly taxed. To tax the immediate capital gains of the stock would be double taxation. Thus with comprehensive taxation of business income at the source, capital gains should be excluded from taxation at the household level.

In order to impose the appropriate tax on banks and certain other types of business, it is necessary to separate the value of the service the bank provides to its customers from the interest the bank pays to the customer. Today, most banks net one against the other, so the customer gets free services in exchange for lending the bank funds at zero or below-market interest rates. Because the business tax would be imposed on the value of the product sold by a business (the services provided by a bank, for example), but would not allow a deduction for interest paid out, it would not be permissible for a bank to report the net receipts from its customers as its sales. Instead, it must add in the difference between the interest it pays its depositors and the full market interest rate they could earn elsewhere. Businesses would not be permitted to borrow from their customers and pretend that the value of sales was only the net charge after deducting interest. This violates the basic principle that interest payments are never deductible. Businesses, like banks, could continue to deal with their customers in any way they chose, but for tax purposes, the full value of their services would be reported as their sales.

Another potential source of abuse of the business tax would need to be monitored: the conversion of business assets to personal use. There is nothing new about this problem. Under today's income tax, one can buy a car for business purposes at the end of the year, take the investment credit, and then convert the car to personal use at the beginning of the next year. Under the proposed business tax, conversion to personal use would be counted as a sale, and the market value of the asset would be included in the revenue of the firm. Auditors would check that the firm's assets were actually used by the firm and not for the personal use of the owners.

First-year write-off of investment would create large tax losses in the start-up years for almost all businesses and occasional large tax losses even for established businesses when they made significant investments. The business tax provides unlimited carry-forward of tax losses so that taxes are reduced in future, profitable years. Further, the balances carried forward earn interest at the market rate.

THE COMPENSATION TAX

Most income in the United States is compensation for work. We propose that compensation be taxed at the level of the individual or married couple. Compensation is defined as cash wages, salaries, and pensions received by workers from employers. Pension contributions and other fringe benefits paid by employers are not counted as part of compensation.

To limit the tax burden of poor families, we propose a set of personal allowances. Taxes would be 19 percent of compensation in excess of personal allowances. The proposed allowances for 1985 are:

Married couple	$9,000
Single individual	4,500
Single head of household	8,000
Each dependent	1,800

Except for the personal allowances, no deductions of any kind would be permitted, including interest deductions.

The tax return for the compensation tax would fit on a postcard (Fig. 7.2).

In 1981 wages, salaries, and private pensions totaled about $1,503 billion. We estimate that personal allowances in 1981 would have been $481 billion, leaving taxable compensation of $1,022 billion. At a rate of 19 percent, tax revenues would have been $194 billion. By

Figure 7.2 *Hall-Rubushka Simplified Flat-Rate Tax Form*

Form 1	Individual Wage Tax	1985
Your first name and initial of joint return (also give spouse's name and initial)	Last name	Your social security number
Present home address (Number and street including apartment number or rural route)		Spouse's social security no.
City, Town or Post Office, State and ZIP Code	Your occupation / Spouse's occupation	

1 Wages and Salary	1	
2 Pensions	2	
3 Total *(line 1 plus line 2)*	3	
4 Personal allowance		
(a) ☐ $9000 for married filing jointly	4(a)	
(b) ☐ $4500 for single	4(b)	
(c) ☐ $8000 for single head of household	4(c)	
5 Number of dependents, not including spouse	5	
6 Personal allowances for dependents *(line 5 multiplied by $1800)*	6	
7 Total personal allowances *(line 4 plus line 6)*	7	
8 Taxable wages *(line 3 less line 7, if positive, otherwise zero)*	8	
9 Tax *(19% of line 8)*	9	
10 Tax withheld by employer	10	
11 Tax due *(line 9 less line 10, if positive)*	11	
12 Refund due *(line 10 less line 9, if positive)*	12	

comparison, the personal income tax in 1981 yielded about $289 billion. The required revenue from the compensation tax is less than from the personal income tax it replaces because the business tax covers part of the tax base of the current personal tax. The reasons that a low rate of 19 percent yields revenue reasonably close to that obtained from the current tax system are: (1) the business tax includes currently untaxed fringes in its base; (2) the current income tax fails to tax fully dividends, interest, and other forms of business income because of widespread evasion and avoidance; and (3) the current tax allows a number of deductions not included in our proposal, the most important of which is the deduction of state and local taxes.

BALANCING THE BUDGET WITH A SIMPLE TAX

If federal spending can be held to the level proposed by President Reagan in his budget for the 1983 fiscal year, or if any increases can be financed by user fees or earmarked taxes, then the 19 percent tax rate would balance the budget by 1985. Even if spending is at the high level projected in the Congressional Budget Office's baseline budget, a tax rate of 19 percent would bring the federal deficit down to $75 billion by 1987.

Under the President's spending proposals, the tax rates necessary to balance the budget starting in fiscal year 1983 would be 21 percent in that year, 20 percent in 1984, and 19 percent in 1985. Under the higher CBO baseline spending projections, the tax rates necessary to balance the budget would be 23 percent in 1983 and 1984, 22 percent in 1985, 21 percent in 1986, and 20 percent in 1987. Immediate adoption of the simple tax would bring moderate deficits during the current recession, but it would commit the nation to a balanced budget within three years, provided spending is kept at reasonable levels.

The base for the simple tax is gross national product less indirect business taxes and investment. In arriving at our conclusions, we used projections of the GNP from the President's budget and from the CBO. We approximated the base as 79 percent of the GNP, based on detailed calculations for 1980.

The simple tax allows each taxpaying individual or family to deduct a personal allowance. These allowances would be indexed according to the cost of living from the proposals for 1985. The total allowance for a husband, wife, and two children in 1985 would be $12,600. Our estimates of total allowances were derived from our estimate for 1981 by assuming one percent annual growth in the number of taxpayers and rates of increase of the cost of living from the President's budget and from the CBO baseline projections.

The simple tax replaces the personal and corporate taxes, but not the rest of the federal tax system, of which the Social Security payroll tax is by far the most important part. Our computations take a projection of total federal spending less a projection of revenue from the other taxes. If the simple tax yields exactly this amount of revenue, it would just balance the budget.

The computations take account of the influence of past deficits on current spending through the interest on the national debt. We used the projections of the Treasury-bill interest rate underlying the President's budget and the CBO projections in order to track the effect of a reduced national debt on interest expense.

We do not attempt to take account of the influence of tax reform on total economic activity and the corresponding augmentation of federal revenue, although these effects could be substantial.

THE FUTURE OF THE ECONOMY UNDER THE SIMPLE INCOME TAX

At the outset, the simple income tax, with common flat rates of 19 percent on business income and compensation, would raise revenue equal to about 12 percent of the GNP, the same as the current combination of corporate and personal income taxes. The personal allowances under our proposed tax system would be raised from year to year in line with inflation, which would tend to hold its revenue constant as a fraction of the GNP. (The new law provides for this kind of indexation starting in 1985.)

The switch from the current corporate and personal income taxes to the simple income tax would have some mild transitional effects on the U.S. economy. Briefly, the elimination of depreciation deductions for business would be costly to the owners of existing plant and equipment, but this would be largely offset by the reduction in the taxation of the earnings of capital assets. We do not think any special compensation is necessary for the loss.

Adoption of the simple tax would lower interest rates. Rates would fall immediately because investors would require a lower rate of interest when they were no longer paying tax on the interest. In the medium run, the investment boom set off by the more favorable tax treatment of capital formation might bring interest rates partway back to their earlier level. In the long run, interest rates would decline as capital accumulation proceeded. Prices of bonds would rise as soon as the tax was announced. None of these effects would be large, and none seems to call for any corrective action by the government. Compared to the gigantic capital losses inflicted on bondholders by inflation and rising taxes over the past decade, and the corresponding capital gains accruing to homeowners over the same period, neither of which has been offset by any government policy, the effects of the simple tax in the opposite direction are mild.

Although our system will stabilize revenue as a fraction of the GNP, it will probably produce more revenue than the government needs to maintain existing programs. Low marginal tax rates will draw economic activities from the underground economy into the formal market, where they are recorded as part of the GNP. Businesses and individuals will spend less time worrying about the tax consequences of their actions and will concentrate instead on earning higher incomes. On these grounds, we believe that the revenue needs of the federal government could be met with tax rates as low as 16 or 17 percent, rather than the 19 pecent needed to reproduce current revenue at current levels of the GNP.

Over the postwar period, cuts in marginal tax rates have coincided with episodes of vigorous economic growth and reduced inflation in the United States. Moreover, those nations with lower marginal tax rates have achieved the highest economic growth over the past decade. The growth stimulated by tax reform is not only favorable for the increased income it would bring to the American public, but it would also moderate and eventually eliminate the federal budget deficit.

The benefits of tax reform are not purely economic. The complexities of the federal tax system foster contempt for government and make petty criminals out of a large fraction of the population. A simplified tax with low marginal rates would help restore confidence in government and would support the basic honesty of the American people.

8 Democratic Procedures and Tax Policy

John F. Witte

The images that best reflect the essence of tax politics have changed considerably in recent years. My explorations lead to an image of tax politics that is highly consistent with what one would predict and applaud as emerging from a pluralist-incremental system. I suspect that both the populist image of tax politics as a tightly controlled agenda benefiting the wealthy and economically powerful and the conservative image of the income tax as an American version of redistributive socialism designed to destroy a meritocratic distribution of rewards are radically overdrawn.

The process of enacting taxes, far from being a sweep toward either of the goals implied by these interpretations, is instead a tedious, complicated process of continuous change involving many actors, and it shifts with circumstances and changes in political-power relationships in an effort to balance contradictory sets of values. Most of the key actors are capable experts, willing to compromise and, when necessary, capable of putting the general interest ahead of more parochial, self-serving interests. Further, the results of this "muddling through," while not fully satisfactory to any specific set of interests

---

This chapter is based on the concluding chapter of the author's *The Politics and Development of the Federal Income tax* (Madison: University of Wisconsin Press, 1985).

or to any particular tax theory, are a politically acceptable combination of policies that match the range of demands placed on the system. The tax code could be viewed as a versatile and flexible policy tool, readily conforming to changing needs and changing political will.

I am convinced that the incremental model applies to most of the tax-policy decisions and that the policy-making process is pluralistic in terms of both the number of actors and the range of interests represented. The actors for the most part are not devious or obsessed with power, but rather seem to be conscientious politicians moved by predictable incentives. I am equally certain that the extreme liberal and conservative images are both distorted. Tax politics has not been dominated solely by the wealthy in a quiet conspiracy to undo a democratically wrought leveling policy. On the other hand, if tax politics is projected as a left-wing march toward a redistributive ethic, the path is totally obscure to me.

However, several generic problems with pluralist-incremental decision making seriously erode this positive image. The root of the problem is the important value incrementalists place on change and adjustment. Incrementalism is lauded for its ability to shift policy directions, either to meet new demands or to correct ineffective policy efforts. Some proponents also argue that through a series of incremental attacks on a problem major changes can be introduced without the problems associated with centralized, planned change.

However, the incessant pressure for change also has a number of serious negative effects that are seldom discussed. It creates instability that confuses citizens and makes it difficult for citizens and organizations to anticipate the future shape of laws. More important, if tax policy is any indicator, the pressure for change and the inability of the political process to resist it facilitate the creation of a legal structure that is immensely complex, one that threatens the capacity of government by inducing and indulging claims that extend beyond resource limits and spreads the actions of government so thin that the central policy goals are often lost as the tangle of programs and provisions grows. This chapter will analyze both the positive aspects of the democratic process in tax politics and the more pathological policy outcomes resulting from the incremental process of change.

PROCESS EFFECTIVENESS

Political decisions that fulfill most of the theoretical criteria of democratic policy making (as described by the pluralist-incremental paradigm) may produce unpleasant policy outcomes when extended over a long period. As a single policy case, income tax policy is particularly relevant because of the widespread belief that the problems that have emerged in tax policy result from a perversion and distortion of democratic procedures. On the contrary, the decision-making procedures generally fit the theoretical description, but the policy results are still troublesome. The implication is unsettling.

Analysis of procedural democracy occurs at several levels of abstraction. Procedural democracy in the broadest sense is related to the role of elections and elite and party competition. In its most rigorous form, informed voters apply either projective judgment of the promises or retrospective judgment of the actions of individual candidates. In the projective form, voters must know their minds on a particular issue, have information concerning the proposed actions of candidates, and fit these two positions together to make their choice. In retrospective voting a similar fit is proposed, but it is based this time not on promised actions, but on actions taken by incumbents. The attitudinal evidence suggests that voters have great difficulty in meeting the rigorous requirements of either of these models in a field as complex as tax policy. This is certainly the case if one expects judgment to be based on details of tax policy and if the object of that judgment is a congressional candidate. However, at least in recent years, the population has generally seen the presidential candidates as embodying broad policy differences. Moreover, at least in 1972 and 1980, these perceptions were based on real differences between the candidates; and in the latter case, the tax issue was critical, and the political system responded to this message.

A more realistic yet still very general model of procedural democracy assumes that political party labels provide information on either projected policy positions of individual candidates. Whether representation is adequate depends on whether parties adequately represent different positions, and that depends on the shape of the underlying distribution of attitudes. If attitudes cluster around one position, parties will project similar stances; if attitudes are dispersed, party positions must be differentiated to accommodate the diversity. If attitudes are complex or unclear, it is difficult to judge the appropriate representative requirement for party positions.

For tax policy it is difficult to assess the adequacy of party representation based on these requirements. Judging from the handful of surveys that ask people to indicate where they believed political parties stood on tax issues, it appears that most people perceive a substantial difference between parties on the issues of tax cutting (in 1980) and progressivity (1972, 1976). However, on both of these issues, those who place themselves at the extremes on the scales are more numerous than those who perceive either party as holding its own position. More troublesome perhaps is that the expected differences in party actions are generally not borne out in practice. Although peak conflicts and the rhetoric of tax politics serve to separate the parties in the anticipated directions, the engine of tax politics is bipartisan agreement on general trends and a reciprocal spreading of tax benefits to broad sets of constituents. Both parties normally support tax reduction and increasing and expanding tax expenditures, and both exhibit ambivalence or distaste toward anything other than mildly progressive effective rates. However, there is also evidence, though not totally conclusive, that the majority of the population supports these trends, and therefore it is difficult to fault the parties for their similarities. In this respect the misperceptions of party differences are harmless illusions in that party actions are more attuned to public wishes than the public is aware. Undoubtedly a multiparty system would better capture the nuances and extremes in public attitudes, but this is true for all policy areas, and the two-party system's countervailing benefits—stability, decisiveness, and moderation—apply as they have applied for over a century in such debates.

Discussions of procedural democracy also occur at a more basic level of discourse that revolves around the actual procedures followed in the decision-making process. The criteria for judging the process at this level include the openness and thoroughness of deliberations, whether individual decisions and stances are publicly recorded, the distribution of power among decision makers, and the adequacy of access for those wishing to petition them. On each of these scores, the tax-policymaking process is much better than prevailing images suggest, and there is evidence, at least for the first three of these criteria, that the situation has improved dramatically in recent years. Most meetings are now open and seemingly endless; the rate of voting, both in committees and on the floor, has increased considerably; and the power of committee chairmen has been greatly diminished in the aftermath of congressional reforms. That these procedural "advances" have been accompanied by a rapid deterioration of the tax base, an increasing tax-expenditure system, and a dramatic increase will be discussed below.

The availability of access and the distribution of influence across affected groups are much harder to judge. Influence is difficult to define and even more difficult to observe and measure. My studies indicate that the wealthy and corporations have obvious influence on tax policy, but also that special deference is shown to the middle class and that all taxpayers—and many nontax-payers—benefit to a considerable extent from the special provisions that provide exemptions, exclusions, deductions, credits, and preferences. Although access and influence may not be perfectly balanced, they are not confined to a particular set of interests. Thus, although the procedural aspects of tax policy are far from perfect, some aspects are positive both in terms of criteria of representation of policy positions, and requirements of the decision-making process.

POLICY OUTCOMES: A PATHOLOGY OF TAX POLITICS

There is one troubling fact that affects judgment of tax systems, particularly if we consider attitudes of taxpayers as one measure of success of failure: No one really likes taxes, and almost everyone can justify personal complaints against the taxes he or she pays. If this is so, and I have little reason to doubt the proposition, one's judgment of the tax system should take this into consideration. One conclusion could be that it does a basically ugly job as well as we can reasonably expect. Following this line of reasoning, broad dissatisfaction with the "fairness" of the system is what one would expect and is a poor indicator of the overall inadequacy of the income tax system. This argument has a seductive appeal, particularly for practical-minded realists who charge that academics apply ivory-tower expectations to policy problems.

However, I sense that resentment toward the tax system goes beyond intellectual nitpicking and runs deeper than the excessive political rhetoric that surrounds periodic calls for reform. There is something self-destructive in the development of the income tax, something that after many years led Wilbur Mills to describe the tax code as a "house of horrors." Over the years, in trying to respond to the demands of diverse groups, to meet the political needs of decision makers and, most important, to correct, adjust, and fine-tune the system, the income tax as a fundamental and ostensibly equitable means of raising revenue has been slowly but continuously eroded. In the process, any possibility of using the tax system to redistribute income now or in the future has been lost. What has emerged may be a versatile and flexible policy tool, but it is also a devastatingly complex tangle of diverse legislative provisions and administrative rules.

Complexity

The difficult problem to grapple with in tax policy is that complexity usually derives from well-intentioned actions and very natural political reactions. This is why everyone complains about the problem, but it gets progressively worse. In budget politics a program often starts out small and gradually increases, a strategy aptly described by Professor Aaron Wildavsky as "the wedge of the nose of the camel." There is a direct parallel in tax policy. However, expansion is seldom a matter of simply shifting numbers and readjusting budget allocations (it may not be that simple for direct subsidy programs either). Rather the expansion, whether in a rate, amount, or time parameter or an eligibility category, often entails rewriting categories or provisions either to safeguard the original recipients to tailor the new benefits to fit a precise set of circumstances or to avoid abuse. Thus, for example, when IRAs were expanded, they were first extended to specific groups of nonprofit workers (which had to be carefully defined), then they were extended to meet very specialized segments of the work force that were not covered by formal pension plans, and finally, when they were extended in reduced form to everyone, further special provisions were added to cover the work of house spouses. As a teacher, I believe

I am presently eligible for three different types of IRAs, although I am not sure.

Complexity also results from efforts to control abuse. Business deductions for costs incurred in the production or sale of goods have always been an integral part of the tax system, but so have the yachts, hunting lodges, airplanes, and extravagant entertainment deductions of a small minority. Provisions and rules that draw a legal line are complicated and continually challenged by new situations. Most would agree that nonprofit, charitable foundations should be tax-exempt, but what if they cover revenue-generating activities or provide a means to pay exorbitant salaries and fringe benefits that in other businesses would be converted into profit? Real-estate provisions, such as accelerated depreciation, inflated interest deductions, and various credits can all be traced to a desire either to stimulate an industry or to meet a particular housing need. However, when they also serve to shelter the income of the very wealthy and in the process distort the original policy intent, complex lines need to be drawn defining a maximum of loss that can be claimed and a minimum amount of taxes that must be paid. In all these cases, the original rationale stands, and thus so does the incentive to keep the provision. The solution is to patch the code, to encircle the abuse with restrictions, limits, and extra conditions. The by-product of these rational actions is extraordinary complexity.

A genuine desire for horizontal equity, defined on a case-by-case basis rather than universally, also produces complexity. For example, we want to take into account extraordinary outlays for such things as medical expenses or casualty losses, but we also want to make certain that such expenditures really hurt. The amount of hurt depends on the amount of income; thus floors are established as a percentage of income; ceilings may be imposed as well. Similarly, although most would approve exempting from taxation income transferred to those assumed to be needy (such as unemployment compensation, Social Security benefits, and retirement income), is it fair to others if those receiving such income also have much more? To correct this inequity, income levels, partial exclusions, and phased-out exemptions are created.

Finally, complexity has followed in the wake of the tax code's expansion as both a general and a refined policy tool. The resulting provisions are not only abundant but also complex in their own right. Alternative-energy devices fall into a number of categories, each of which must be defined—and defined carefully, so that home additions with numerous windows do not receive solar-energy credits. The definitions, amounts of credits, and categories will also undoubtedly shift as energy conditions shift. Often they remain past their useful life because, as in direct subsidy systems, attentive and persistent interest groups and industries have become accustomed to their presence. The cumulative effect as more areas are incorporated is ever-increasing complexity.

Redistribution

That the income tax fails to redistribute income in any real sense could be cited as a point in its favor in that actual effective rates closely approximate the mean rates people believe different income groups should pay. However, the matter is not that simple. Attitudes are not all that clear; simple conclusions camouflage ambiguity, uncertainty, and inconsistency. Many policy experts from various points on the political spectrum would support a redistributive system, probably based on a negative income tax, in preference to the present array of direct government programs to deal with economic need and poverty. But we have no public-opinion data on that option. And one cannot overlook the fact that some notion of vertical equity, progressivity, ability to pay, or simple redistribution has always been at the center of tax discussions, particularly discussions of the merits of the income tax. Finally, and what may be ultimately the telling outcome: Not only has the tax system failed to redistribute income, but even if future attitudes should support such a program, the politics and structure of the income tax make redistribution an unlikely prospect.

There are a number of interrelated factors that render the income tax impotent as a tool of redistribution. First, both the historical trends favoring general tax reduction and the deference shown the middle classes have a powerful debilitating effect on the redistributive consequences of tax policy. Given the underlying pretax distribution of income, the level of taxation would have to be very large to affect the overall distribution, even if the effective tax rates were extremely skewed against the rich.

Similarly, the apparent goal of maintaining stable, essentially proportional effective rates for the middle-class taxpayer would make it difficult to justify the very high rates for upper-income groups that would be necessary to affect redistribution. It also makes it difficult to "shake down" the distribution in progressive steps that would shift some income from the top to the lower half of the distribution. The political rule has been to reduce rates proportionately for everyone but the people at the very ends of the distribution. Changes at the ends vary according to the political and economic environment. Thus the historical notion of equality projected in tax policy over the years has been essentially one of proportional burden, with need compelling lower rates for the very poor and with high rates placed on the wealthy only during periods of crisis.

The nature of the policy-making process is another important reason why the tax system is not used for redistribution purposes. As the income tax developed and grew in scope and complexity, the larger issues of redistribution and class confrontation were lost in the details of legislative battles. This transformation can be explained in part by two developments. The first was that tax bills began to resemble large jigsaw puzzles, the components of which rarely fit a consistent pattern. This meant that individual provisions were treated piecemeal, determined more by their own incremental history than by reference to any standard of redistribution. If progressivity was a factor at all, it was only one among many.

The second explanation, not totally unrelated to the first, was that as the tax expenditure system grew, the problem of redistribution, which was often raised in connection with rate changes, was displaced in importance by tax-expenditure debates that were essentially distributive in nature. The discussion shifted from consideration of relative advantages to debates over specific needs and desired actions. The elderly on fixed incomes are suffering, the building industry is in the worst slump since the Depression, we need to stimulate energy exploration, and so on. As the use of the tax code for varying purposes expanded, redistribution simply took a backseat to distributive requirements based on need or incentive effects.

Complexity of the tax code also affects its redistributive properties and potential. A policy structure that resembles a large briar bush is difficult to prune. A cornerstone of incrementalism is the ability to effect remedial change to correct policy errors or move in new directions.

A final factor preventing redistribution is more speculative and difficult to state in an analytically rigorous manner. Tax policy has reflected an ambivalent and equivocating attitude toward redistribution. However, one aspect of that ambivalence is the almost total lack of a *positive ideal of equality.* Almost always the arguments for progressivity have been based either on revenue needs or on the privileged position of the wealthy. The beneficial effects of equality are seldom presented, rather, the arguments are instrumental or simply vindictive. Wars provided the major instrumental rationale, whereas reform legislation was often introduced, as in 1969, by a symbolic attack on abuse, such as pillorying a few wealthy individuals who pay no taxes. Since instrumental conditions change and a belief in meritocracy seems to be well ingrained in the American psyche, both bases for equality have proved to be short-lived.

Revenue Capacity

In the early postwar period the tax base expanded because of rising incomes and presidential resistance to tax reduction. During this period most of the erosion of the tax base was the result of tax exemptions and income exclusions (primarily transfer payments). As incomes increased and the middle-class shelters provided by exemptions, exclusions, and the standard deduction were reduced, the tax base expanded, but so did the drive for tax expenditures. By 1969 the tax base had begun to shrink. Inflationary growth in income in the 1970s cemented these trends and culminated in the 1981 tax cut and indexing provisions. Tax expenditures have taken on a more significant role for the middle class, and barring steep reductions in the personal exemptions, which have traditionally been only lowered in wartime and presently are covered by indexing provisions, the tax base is likely to continue to decline. If the indexing of rates is allowed to take effect as planned—and terrific political pressure will be needed to prevent it—the income tax will eventually lose its capacity to provide necessary revenues. Even with the modest increase in tax revenues legislated in 1982 (mostly by tightening administrative provisions), projected deficits for the foreseeable future are on the order of $200 billion per year, or about 5 percent of the GNP. Since the underlying trends, incentives, and decision-making processes that led to this result are well entrenched, the politics of income taxation apparently follows a self-destructive path.

REMEDIES, REGRESSIONS, AND REMISSIONS

The Inadequacy of Tax Reform

At first glance, the remedy for these pathologies of the tax system appears to be obvious, if not altogether original. The answer would seem to be a major tax-reform effort along standard comprehensive tax baselines, with whatever blend of progressivity in rates the political process might dictate. A stack of such reform schemes is readily available from all corners of the political spectrum. One set of proposals falls under the generic term "flat tax." Most would eliminate most tax expenditures and compress the nominal rate structure. The latest and most prominent is the Hall-Rabushka scheme to reduce the personal income tax form to a postcard allowing (unspecified) business deductions and little else and requiring only twelve lines of information. Income would then be taxed at a single rate close to the current effective rate paid by the broad middle-income groups (12 to 14 percent). The Bradley-Gephardt proposal would have three rate levels and allow deductions for mortgage interest, taxes, charitable contributions, and payments into IRAs and Keogh plans. Interestingly, few of these proposals discuss excluded forms of income or indirect wages in the form of employee contributions to health insurance, retirement plans, and so on.

Other reform proposals also consider corporate changes. The most grandoise is the Treasury Department's 1977 *Blueprints for Basic Tax Reform,* which outlines a master plan for eliminating many tax expenditures and at the same time integrates the individual and corporate taxes. This proposal has been cited less in the last several years as attention has shifted to the flat tax and a revived expenditure tax, which would be based on a reformed income tax that excludes savings. The latter, which comes in several administrative varieties, has been offered as an addition to the income tax or, more often, as a substitute for it. All these major reforms begin with the premise that the income tax system is in dire straits. I agree with the premise, but I am bewildered and some what bemused by the remedies.

There is absolutely nothing in the history or politics of the income tax that indicates that any of these schemes have the slightest hope of being enacted in the forms proposed. In fact, if the past is any guide, reform efforts, whether radical proposals like those above or more modest changes of an incremental variety, are likely to aggravate the problem over the long run. People and institutions have memories; reforms in one political period are likely to be followed by counter-attacks on the tax system in another. Although the reforms might temporarily increase revenues and positively affect redistribution, the few reform bills that have been enacted have had only the slightest impact on these problems when viewed in historical perspective. The main result has been more complexity, which in turn provides more numerous and less visible targets for those seeking specialized tax relief in a later period.

Insulating Policy from Politics

The answer is not to reform the tax system or even to seek immediate policy remedies, but rather to alter the political process to prevent even further regression. The general goal should be, as Professor Allen Schick has compellingly argued, to restore non-decision making—to change the politics of taxation so as to retard and stabilize change. Thus the goal should be to seek not remedies, but merely a remission from the malady. And that requires political, not policy, reform.

Dr. Joseph A. Pechman, who has studied, analyzed, and worried about the tax system for a good many years, has also come to the conclusion that political reform is the key. However, his solution, which he implies would usher in a tax-reform era, is to reform election laws to provide public financing for congressional candidates, thus freeing them from the clutches of special-interest groups. If my analysis is correct, this proposal falls far short. Money from any source is only one of the pressures forcing members of Congress to "produce" for their constituents. And for tax politics it is probably a minor consideration when compared with the pressures generated by the large middle class, which dines along with the rich, the poor, and the special-interest groups at the tax-benefit table. Freeing representatives from the burdens of electoral financing may prevent some tax abuse, but it will not prevent the wholesale erosion of the base that comes from income and fringe-benefit exclusions, deduction of taxes, interest, the exemption of IRA funds, and broad-based corporate provisions that purportedly aid the economy and indisputably aid large numbers in the business community. And we must assume that the ingenuity of elected politicians in devising new methods to confer such benefits is unlimited. The answer is not to reform the representative process, but to insulate policy from it.

Those words do not come easily for one raised in a pluralist tradition, and undoubtedly they will be challenged by many. What is implied is that democracy must be contained—that it must be tempered to prevent elected officials from offering constituents, in good conscience, what those constituents want. The underlying malady is the *hyperresponsiveness* of the system. It is not that the "electoral connection" is too loose or disjointed; it is that it is too much tied to personal interests, too shortsighted, and too often exercised. Decisions that appear rational and proper in each individual case are in the aggregate and over time a disaster.

An obvious first step is to repeal the reforms enacted in Congress in the early 1970s, at least as they apply to the tax committees. These reforms assumed that a more open process with broader participation would lead to more responsible actions, in that efforts to cater to narrow interests would be overruled or would be exposed to political attack. Under the new rules the interests catered to often turned out to be broad ones, but even if they were not, public access, rather than discouraging tax benefits, actually provided politicians with a convenient and appealing platform that they could use to take credit for the measures in a bill that aided their particular constituents. Some initial reforms would be the restoration of the power of the committee chairmen, reduction of the size of committees, and perhaps even the establishment of a subcommittee of the House Ways and Means and Finance Committees to deal with income tax legislation. The closed rule limiting floor debate on a tax bill should be reinstituted and extended to the Senate. Finally, open committee sessions should be restricted and confined to the early stages of a bill.

Although these changes might restore some order to the legislative process and establish some control over tax spending, the basic incentive structure remains. One way to alter those incentives, at least during conservative periods, is to tie tax-expenditure decisions to direct spending, thus attaching the stigma of the latter to the former. In the Canadian format, tax and spending decisions are placed in the same functional "envelope," so that when any program is discussed, whether a tax program or a direct expenditure, the relevant provisions and estimated budget effects are analyzed together. However, the one modest effort to institute such a procedure in 1976 was soundly defeated on the Senate floor.

The other way to solve the incentive problem is to circumvent Congress altogether. So long as members of Congress perceive their tasks and their records as being tied to the generation of both broad and specialized legislative benefits, the historical trends in tax politics will persist. And although popular perceptions of Congress as an institution have remained extremely unfavorable in recent years, the high reelection rates of incumbents must be reinforcing previous behavior. Thus, so long as tax politics remains the prerogative of Congress, the underlying pressures to use the tax code to distribute benefits and offer solutions to specific policy problems will be enormous, regardless of the institutional changes that are made. Therefore, the critical reform must be the insulation of tax decisions from politics, either by creating legal moratoriums that prevent changes in the tax system or by shifting decisions to administrative bodies and executive agencies.

The former strategy has been suggested by Joseph Pechman, who nevertheless clings to reform hopes. He recommends a five-year hiatus between "reform efforts," which would be guided by an assemblage of experts. The legal or institutional basis for such a moratorium is not clear, however. Proposals to shift decision-making power to the executive branch and to administrative agencies are less common, although there are precedents in related policy fields and in the income tax systems of other industrialized countries.

The history of U.S. tariff policy is such a precedent and provides a striking parallel to the problems currently faced by the income tax. Early tariff legislation consumed similar amounts of time and generated the high levels of consternation that have characterized income tax legislation in recent years. In the wake of the 1929–30 Smoot-Hawley Tariff debacle, stimulated by the Democratic landslide and by the Roosevelt Administration in the person of Cordell Hull, then Secretary of State and an unabashed free-trader, Congress enacted the 1934 Reciprocal Trade Agreements act, which removed tariff decisions from Congress, empowering the executive branch to negotiate tariff changes up to 50 percent of existing rates. The negotiated results were to take the form of executive orders and not treaties, which would have required congressional approval.

There are also precedents in other countries for this manner of insulation of tax policy from politics—countries that remain viable democracies. In both Germany and Canada, to take two well-documented cases, tax decisions are centralized in the executive branch, which serves as both the initiating arm for legislation and a powerful filter for proposals that originate elsewhere. On the other hand, British tax legislation is enacted in an open environment very similar to that in the United States, and the results are also similar.

To what degree a shift in tax power from the legislative to the executive branch would stabilize tax policy is an open question. However, peacetime experience indicates that the executive branch has generally maintained greater restraint than Congress. The Mellon Treasury, while reducing taxes steadily in the 1920s, initiated reductions prudently, only following government surpluses. And when it was decided that revenue was needed to balance the budget, Mellon and the Roosevelt Administration cooperated with Congress in raising taxes in 1932. Most of the administration's initiatives, however symbolic, were geared to increase taxes and close loopholes. After World War II Truman alone resisted tax reduction, finally succumbing to a congressional override in 1948. And the Eisenhower Administration followed suit, holding the line on tax changes for eight years, despite pressures from both parties to reduce taxes during recessions. Since World War II, as the executive branch has asserted itself more in tax matters, its suggestion for changes in the code have been more balanced than Congress's. Even for the monumental Economic Recovery Tax Act of 1981, the initial administration proposals were extremely modest relative to the congressional add-ons of both parties.

In addition to the historical case, a logical argument can be made for greater executive influence. After four years in office, presidents have much more difficulty than congressmen in avoiding responsibility for economic failure. Although presidents try mightily to put the blame for economic problems on an uncooperative Congress or bureaucracy, international events, or simply time lags, evasion of responsibility is difficult, and the audiences to which they must appeal are very broad. Congressmen, on the other hand, can shift attention from the larger issues to the particularistic benefits provided to constituents, and they can avoid blame by pleading impotence, blaming the administration, or by running against Congress itself. To the extent that tax changes adversely affect economic conditions—and deficits are the most obvious problem—presidential responsibility for these conditions indicates tax restraints that may not exist for Congress. However, the next few years may be critical in this respect. If a Republican is reelected easily in 1984 and if the economy is particularly strong, there is no question that the President will claim that tax initiatives were mainly responsible. Barring a renewal of fear of deficits (a renewal that seems certain as this is written), a Reagan reelection might reverse the logic above and set a different course for future aspirants to that office. In that event, the tax system would be a slow-moving and wide-open target for all, and even a dramatic shift in power from Congress to the executive branch would be ineffectual in saving the tax system.

The prospects of such political changes depend more on the course of future political and economic events than on either past actions or intellectual analysis. If indexing goes into effect and deficits persist, and if deficits are linked politically to the economic malaise, something will be done. The system has adapted in the past, and the capacity to do so remains. Whether the adaptation will be toward a new type of tax, marginal increases in existing taxes, or a change in the political process in the directions I have suggested is anyone's guess. Although the historical policy trends and current political incentives and institutional arrangements all seem to point to the need for political reform, the link between representation and taxes is constitutionally and ideologically ingrained as a sacred right. We may well end up simply paying a higher price for that right than was originally expected.

APPENDIX

The Treasury Tax Reform Plan

INTRODUCTORY COMMENT

The Treasury Department submitted the comprehensive tax reform plan summarized in this appendix to the President of the United States on November 27, 1984. The plan deals with all the deficiencies of the federal income taxes described in chapter 1. It proposes to eliminate most of the unnecessary and inefficient deductions, credits, and tax preferences in the individual and corporation income taxes, and uses the revenues to reduce the tax rates. It provides for indexation of incomes from capital and eliminates the huge distortions in the taxation of firms in different industries. It also simplifies the tax system, particularly for the low and middle income taxpayers.

For individuals, the Treasury plan doubles the personal exemptions, reduces personal deductions, curtails tax-free fringe benefits (other than pensions), and eliminates the capital gains preference. Interest on future issues of private-purpose tax-exempt bonds would be subject to tax. A simple three-bracket tax rate structure of 15, 25, and 35 percent would replace the present 14 brackets ranging from 11 to 50 percent.

For corporations, the investment tax credit and the Accelerated Cost Recovery System of depreciation are replaced by economic depreciation adjusted for inflation. Special preferences for the oil and gas industry and financial institutions are eliminated. The corporate rate would be reduced to a flat 33 percent.

The Treasury Tax Reform Plan

The present U.S. tax system desperately needs simplification and reform. It is too complicated, it is unfair, and it retards savings, investment, and economic growth.

Under the current progressive tax system, all taxpayers face higher marginal tax rates in order to make up for the revenue lost by numerous special preferences, exceptions, and tax shelters used by a relatively small number of taxpayers.

As a result, the tax system is complex and inequitable. It reduces economic incentives, hampers economic growth, and is perceived to be so unfair that taxpayer morale and voluntary compliance have been seriously undermined.

As requested by President Reagan in his 1984 State of the Union Address, the Treasury Department has completed a thorough review of the U.S. tax system. This summary outlines the Department's proposals for a fundamental reform and simplification of the income tax system which would raise approximately the same amount of revenues as current law with lower tax rates imposed on a broader tax base.

The Treasury Department is proposing a new income tax system which is broad-based, simple, and fair. It

---

This chapter is based on the summary chapter of the U.S. Treasury's study, *Tax Reform for Fairness, Simplicity and Economic Growth* (Office of the Secretary of the Treasury, November 27, 1984), pp. 1–10.

reflects the enormous public input generated by a series of public hearings held throughout the country.

The Treasury Department's recommendation reflects the broad political consensus of the American people that the present system is too complicated and favors special interests at the expense of the general public. While much more comprehensive and far-reaching than other proposals, it resembles several plans for tax reform advanced by members of Congress, especially the Kemp-Kasten and Bradley-Gephardt plans. This bipartisan congressional consensus augurs well for quick action by the Congress.

TAX SIMPLIFICATION AND REFORM FOR INDIVIDUALS

The Treasury Department proposals combine lower tax rates, increased personal exemptions, and zero bracket amounts with the repeal or modification of a number of existing deductions, exclusions and credits. The proposal does not generally change the distribution of individual tax burden across income classes, though it does reduce tax burdens more than proportionally for taxpayers with the lowest incomes.

Rate Structure

The Treasury Department proposal replaces the present 14 brackets of tax rates ranging from 11 to 50 percent with a simple three-bracket system with tax rates set at 15, 25 and 35 percent.

Taxable Income	*Tax Rates (percent)*
Single Persons	
Less than $ 2,800	0
$2,800 to 19,300	15
$19,300 to 38,100	25
$38,100 or more	35

Heads of Household	
Less than $ 3,500	0
$3,500 to 25,000	15
$25,000 to 48,000	25
$48,000 or more	35
Married Couples	
Less than $ 3,800	0
$3,800 to 31,800	15
$31,800 to 63,800	25
$63,800 or more	35

Fairness for Families

In order to provide greater fairness for families, the Treasury Department proposal will increase the personal exemption for all taxpayers and their dependents to $2,000 and increase the zero bracket amounts to $2,800 for singles, $3,800 for joint returns, and $3,500 for heads of households.

These adjustments will virtually eliminate from taxation families with incomes below the poverty level. The individual tax brackets, the personal exemption, and the zero bracket amount would continue to be indexed.

Impact on Individuals

Under the proposal, 78 percent of all taxpayers will experience either no tax change or a tax decrease, and 22 percent will face higher taxes. Of those facing a tax increase, more than half will experience a tax increase of less than one percent of income.

On average, *marginal tax rates will be reduced by about 20 percent and individual tax liabilities will be reduced by an average of 8.5 percent.* Because of the increased tax-free threshold, the average tax reductions are greater at the bottom of the income scale. Tax liabilities of families with incomes below $10,000 will be reduced by an average of 32.5 percent, and the reduction in taxes for families with incomes of $10,000 to $15,000 will be 16.6 percent.

Broadening the Base

In order to broaden the base, simplify the tax system, and eliminate special preferences and abuses, the Treasury Department proposals would modify or repeal a number of itemized deductions, exclusions, and special tax credits.

These changes generally involve special preferences which are not used by the majority of individual taxpayers and include various fringe benefits, wage replacement payments, preferred uses of income, business deductions for personal expenses such as entertainment, and other areas of abuse.

For most taxpayers who do itemize deductions, the marginal rate reductions and the increased personal exemption will offset the benefits lost from the various proposed reforms. However, those taxpayers who consistently make above-average use of deductions and exclusions to shelter their income in order to avoid paying a fair share of the tax burden will face an increase in taxes.

The Treasury Department proposal retains the existing itemized deductions above certain floors for *medical expenses* and for *casualty losses.*

The *home mortgage interest deduction* is retained for a taxpayer's principal residence. Certain other *interest deductions,* including consumer interest and interest on second homes, are allowed up to $5,000 in excess of investment income.

The itemized *deduction for charitable contributions* is retained, but allowed only for charitable contributions in excess of two percent of adjusted gross income.

The deduction for contributions to an *Individual Retirement Account* is retained and increased from $2,000 to $2,500 per employee. The current $250 spousal IRA limit would be increased to $2,500 for spouses working in the home.

The *Social Security benefit exclusion,* which generally excludes from taxation Social Security benefits, would be retained.

The existing *child care credit* would be replaced with a child care deduction.

The *earned income tax credit* would be retained and indexed for inflation.

A new, single *credit* for the *elderly, blind* and *disabled* would be provided, and the current exclusions for workers' compensation and for black lung and certain veterans' disability payments would be folded into the credit.

The *two-earner deduction,* no longer necessary under the revised rate brackets, would be repealed.

The current exclusions for *employer-provided pension and profit-sharing plans* are retained as are the treatment of certain hard-to-value fringe benefits specifically addressed in the Deficit Reduction Act of 1984.

The exclusion of *health insurance benefits* would be retained, but capped at $70 per month for singles and $175 per month for a family. This change would affect only about 30 percent of all employees with such plans.

The special exclusion of *group-term life insurance* and the special treatment of *cafeteria plans* would be repealed, as would the exclusion of *other* employer-provided fringe benefits, such as educational benefits, legal services, and dependent care.

The tax-exempt threshold for *unemployment compensation,* currently set at $18,000 for a joint return, would be repealed. It is not fair that those receiving unemployment compensation pay no tax, while those with equal incomes who work pay tax. With the personal exemption and zero bracket amount increased to $11,800 for a family of four, the impact of this change on low and moderate income taxpayers would be minimal.

Itemized deductions for all *state and local taxes* would be repealed. These deductions are claimed on only a minority of tax returns, and disproportionately benefit higher income individuals in high-tax states and localities.

The use of *business deductions for personal expenses* would be curtailed. Deductions for entertainment would be denied, and deductions for business meals would be limited.

Income Distribution

The Treasury Department proposals are designed to be basically neutral from a distributional point of view. The table below shows that the distribution of individual income tax burdens does not differ significantly from that under current law.

Income Class (000)	Percent of Total Income Taxes Paid: Current Law	Percent of Total Income Taxes Paid: Treasury Proposal
$ 0–10	0.5%	0.3%
10–15	1.8	1.6
15–20	3.3	3.1
20–30	10.3	10.2
30–50	24.3	24.1
50–100	32.8	33.1
100–200	12.3	12.6
200+	14.9	15.0

Average Tax Rates

The proposed tax reforms will reduce individual tax liabilities for all income classes by an average of 8.5 percent. However, those at the bottom of the income scale will receive substantial tax reductions, and those with incomes up to $50,000 will experience above-average reductions in tax liability, as the table below shows.

Income Class (000)	Average Tax Rate by Income Class: Current Law	Average Tax Rate by Income Class: Treasury Proposal	Change
$ 0–10	1.4%	0.9%	−32.5%
10–15	3.2	2.7	−16.6
15–20	4.6	4.0	−12.1
20–30	6.2	5.7	− 9.1
30–50	7.8	7.0	− 9.3
50–100	9.4	8.7	− 7.4
100–200	13.2	12.3	− 6.4
200+	20.9	19.3	− 8.0

Marginal Tax Rates

The Treasury proposal would reduce marginal tax rates by an average of nearly 20 percent. Although marginal tax rates are reduced by a larger percent for those at the top, these income groups will experience smaller than average tax reductions, as shown in the preceding table. Marginal tax rates fall furthest at the top of the income distribution because that is where the tax base is increased by the largest fraction.

Income Class (000)	*Marginal Tax Rate by Income Class*		
	Current Law	*Treasury Proposal*	*Change*
$ 0–10	4.2%	3.7%	−11.9%
10–15	9.4	8.5	− 9.6
15–20	12.4	11.0	−11.3
20–30	16.0	14.0	−12.5
30–50	20.9	16.5	−21.1
50–100	27.6	22.1	−19.9
100–200	37.5	30.5	−18.7
200+	46.1	33.2	−28.0

Tax Simplification

The Treasury proposal repeals or consolidates about 65 provisions in the tax Code. It eliminates the need for at least 16 tax forms and 10 lines from the 1040 form.

The proposed changes will reduce the number of individual taxpayers who itemize their deductions from 36 percent to fewer than 25 percent of all individual taxpayers.

In addition, the Internal Revenue Service is proceeding to develop a *return-free tax system.* Under such a system, the IRS would, at the election of the taxpayer, compute the tax liability of most taxpayers based on withholding and information reports. Institution of a return-free tax system could eliminate the actual filing of tax returns for half or more than half of all taxpayers.

REFORM OF CAPITAL AND BUSINESS INCOME

The taxation of capital and business income in the United States is deeply flawed. It lacks internal consistency, and it is ill-suited to periods when inflation rates have varied and been unpredictable. It contains subsidies to particular forms of investment that distort choices in the use of the nation's scarce capital resources. It provides opportunities for tax shelters that allow wealthy individuals to pay little tax, undermine confidence in the tax system, and further distort economic choices. Equity investment in the corporate sector is placed at a particular disadvantage by the double taxation of dividends. Resulting high marginal tax rates discourage saving, investment, invention, and innovation. Moreover, high marginal rates encourage efforts to obtain additional special tax benefits which, if successful, further erode the tax base and necessitate higher rates in a never-ending cycle.

The Treasury Department's tax reforms would rationalize the taxation of income from business and capital. An overriding objective is to subject real economic income from all sources to the same tax treatment.

Implementation of the reforms proposed by the Treasury Department would cause improved reallocations of economic resources. The lower tax rates made possible by base-broadening and the more realistic rules for the measurement of income and calculation of tax liabilities will increase the attractiveness of industries that suffer under the weight of the current unfair and distortionary tax regime. Both established industries and new "high-tech" industries will benefit from tax reform. But the ultimate beneficiaries will be the American public. No longer will the nation's scarce economic resources—its land, its labor, its capital, and its inventive genius—be allocated by the tax system, instead of by market forces. The result will be more productive investment, greater opportunities for employment, more useful output, and faster economic growth.

Lower Corporate Tax Rates

The Treasury Department's proposals would allow the corporate tax rate to be reduced to 33 percent. All corporations would be subject to this single rate, which is 2 percentage points below the proposed top individual rate.

Capital Gains

Capital gains on assets held for at least a prescribed period have long benefited from preferential tax treatment. Partial exclusion of capital gains has been justified by the need to avoid taxing fictitious gains that merely reflect inflation.

The Treasury Department approach to the inflation problem is more direct—and therefore more equitable and more neutral. Under it the basis (original cost) of assets used in calculating gains would be adjusted for inflation, so that only real gains would be subject to tax. With this inflation adjustment and a rate structure with only a few wide income brackets in place, there would be little need for preferential tax treatment of realized capital gains. Investment in capital assets will continue to enjoy the substantial benefits of deferral of tax until gains are realized. At even moderate rates of inflation, the taxation of real gains as ordinary income at the proposed rates is more generous than the taxation of nominal gains at the current preferential rates. The reduced rates proposed in this report would alleviate any problems of lock-in and bunching.

Capital Consumption Allowances

The investment tax credit (ITC) and the accelerated cost recovery system (ACRS) were introduced to stimulate investment and prevent capital consumption allowances from being eroded by inflation. Since the present tax system does not adjust the basis of depreciable assets for inflation, these provisions were required to prevent confiscatory taxation of income from capital.

At the lower rates of inflation prevailing today, the ITC and ACRS allow investment in depreciable assets to be recovered far more rapidly than under a neutral system of income taxation. As a result, the tax system favors industries that invest heavily in depreciable assets such as equipment over others such as high technology industries, service industries, and the trade sector that invests more heavily in inventories.

Because the advantages of the ITC and ACRS are "front-loaded," these provisions are of relatively little value to new and rapidly growing firms or to ailing industries, neither of which can fully utilize their benefits. New firms are penalized and there are incentives for tax-motivated mergers. The result is reduced competitiveness and less incentive for innovation. The front-loading of tax benefits also leads to the proliferation of tax shelters, many of which are abusive and create severe administrative burdens for the Internal Revenue Service.

To assure that capital consumption allowances will be more nearly appropriate, regardless of the rate of inflation, the Treasury Department proposes that the investment tax credit be repealed, and that the basis of depreciable assets be indexed for inflation, and that depreciation allowances for tax purposes be set to approximate economic depreciation.

Relief for Double Taxation of Dividends

Under present law equity income originating in the corporate sector is taxed twice—first as corporate profits and then as dividends. This double taxation of dividends discourages saving and discriminates against investment in the corporate sector. The Treasury Department proposes that the United States do what many other developed countries do, continue to levy the corporate income tax on earnings that are retained, but provide partial relief from double taxation of dividends. The proposal allows corporations to deduct a portion of the dividends paid out of previously-taxed earnings.

SUBSIDIES FOR SPECIFIC INDUSTRIES

Certain industries benefit from special tax preferences that have no place in a comprehensive income tax. These include the energy and financial sectors. Moreover, the exclusion of interest on bonds issued by state and local governments for private purposes detracts from the fairness of the tax system, as well as distorting capital flows.

Energy

To be consistent with the goal of increased reliance on free-market forces underlying both this Administration's energy policy and these proposals for fundamental tax reform, the Treasury Department proposes that expensing of intangible drilling costs and percentage depletion should be replaced by cost depletion. The proposed rules are identical to proposed changes in the general rules for income measurement for all multi-period production, which require cost capitalization in order to match deductions with taxable receipts.

Consistent with our objective to make the tax system neutral, the Treasury Department proposes to accelerate the phase-out of the Windfall Profits Tax to 1988.

Financial Institutions

The Treasury proposal repeals the preferential tax treatment available to most types of financial institutions. Besides being unfair and distortionary, relative to the taxation of the rest of the economy, these tax preferences create distortions within the financial sector that are inconsistent with the Administration's efforts to deregulate financial markets. Equity and neutrality demand that all financial institutions be taxed uniformly, on all of their net income. These special preferences are especially inappropriate in a world in which the corporate tax rate is lowered and both individuals and other corporations are taxed more nearly on their economic income.

State and Local Government Bonds

Interest on debt issued by state and local governments for public purposes, such as schools, roads and sewers ("public purpose municipal bonds"), has long been exempt from tax. State and local governments have recently expanded the use of tax-exempt bonds in ways that do not have any "public" purpose. Proceeds from tax-exempt bonds have been used for economic development (via industrial development bonds or IDBs), for low-interest mortages on owner-occupied housing, for student loans, and for private hospital and educational facilities. In addition, state and local governments have routinely invested proceeds of tax-exempt bonds in higher-yielding taxable securities to earn arbitrage profits.

The Treasury Department proposal would subject to tax the future issuance of all "private purpose" tax-exempt bonds and tighten the restrictions on arbitrage.

The elimination of private purpose bonds should be of financial benefit to state and local governments. Reducing the volume of tax-exempt bonds will improve the market for public purpose bonds, thus reducing interest costs to governments.

Curtailment of Tax Shelters

As a result of the growth in tax shelter activity, there has been a significant erosion in the base of the Federal income tax, particularly among taxpayers with the highest incomes. Estimates from the 1983 Treasury individual tax model indicate that partnership losses may shelter as much as $35 billion of all individual income from taxation. Roughly 82 percent of this total, or $28.6 billion in partnership losses, were reported by taxpayers with gross incomes (before losses) of $100,000 or more, and 60 percent, or $21.0 billion, were reported by taxpayers with incomes in excess of $250,000. By comparison, these groups reported 9 percent and 4 percent, respectively, of all gross income before losses reported by individuals.

Several of the Treasury Department's proposals—for example, lower tax rates, taxation of real capital gains as ordinary income, capital consumption allowances that approximate economic depreciation, indexing of net interest expense, matching expenses and receipts from multiperiod production, and tax treatment of certain large partnerships as corporations—will greatly reduce the attractiveness of tax shelters. Yet opportunities for tax shelters will remain, and several proposals are being made to further reduce these opportunities.

Contributors

Joseph A. Pechman is Senior Fellow, and formerly Director of Economic Studies, of the Brookings Institution. One of the nation's foremost fiscal economists, he has served as an adviser to presidential candidates and has been a consultant to the Treasury Department, the Council of Economic Advisers, and the Congressional Budget Office. He is the author of *Federal Tax Policy* and *Who Bears the Tax Burden?* and has edited seven books in the Brookings Institution budget series, *Setting National Priorities.*

Henry J. Aaron is a Senior Fellow of the Brookings Institution. He served as Assistant Secretary of Health, Education, and Welfare for Program Planning and Evaluation during the Carter Administration. He is an expert on social economics and budget and tax policy. He is the author of *Politics and the Professors, Economic Effects of Social Security,* and *The Value-Added Tax: Lessons from Europe.*

Bill Bradley is U.S. Senator from New Jersey. He is co-author of the Bradley-Gephardt tax plan and author of *The Fair Tax.*

John E. Chapoton is a member of the law firm of Vinson and Elkins. He served as Assistant Secretary of the Treasury for Tax Policy in the first Reagan Administration.

Harvey Galper is a Senior Fellow of the Brookings Institution. He served as Director of the Office of Tax Analysis, U.S. Treasury Department, from 1976 to 1981. He played a major role in the preparation of *Blueprints for Basic Tax Reform,* a basic reference work on tax policy prepared by the Treasury Department.

Robert E. Hall is Professor of Economics at Stanford University and a Senior Research Fellow of the Hoover Institution. He has written widely on the economic effects of taxation and is co-author of *Low Tax, Simple Tax, Flat Tax.*

Jack Kemp is a member of the U.S. House of Representatives from New York. He is co-author of the Kemp-Kasten tax plan.

Alvin Rabushka is a Senior Research Fellow of the Hoover Institution. He is a political scientist and has specialized on the politics of budget and tax policy. He is co-author of the *Tax Revolt* and of *Low Tax, Simple Tax, Flat Tax.*

John F. Witte is Professor of Political Science at the University of Wisconsin in Madison. He is one of the nation's leading analysts of the tax legislative process and is author of *The Politics and Development of the Federal Income Tax.*

The views expressed in this book are those of the authors and not of the organizations with which they are affiliated.